Inside front cover and above: Leif Eriksson, Norse ruler of Greenland, is believed to have landed here around 1000 A.D. and established America's first European settlement. Located near present-day L'Anse aux Meadows, northern Newfoundland, and unearthed in the 1960s, it was declared a UNESCO World Heritage Site in 1978. Right: The restored remains of a thousand-year-old Norse building near L'Anse aux Meadows, Newfoundland. (Photos: Parks Canada)

Contents

Photos: Christina Sjögren, Erik Svensson, Stig-Göran Nilsson, Anders Jönsson, Thor-Björn Hansson a.o.
Text: Göran Blomé, Lennart Pehrson (The American Dream)
Translation, editing: Victor Kayfetz, Scan Edit, San Francisco
Graphic design: Jan-Erik Ander, Kalinka Sainz, Lexivision AB, Stockholm
Repro: Filmmontörerna, Västerås
Printer: Ljung, Örebro
Binding: Mälardalens Bokbinderi AB
Production: Göran Blomé

© Göran Blomé
BLOMÉDIA AB, Stockholm, Sweden, 1996

ISBN 91-972580-9-1

On location...

Images of Swedish Entrepreneurship in North America

In search of freedom

Frihet är det bästa ting,
som sökas kan all världen kring
för den henne rätt kan bära.
Vill du vara dig själver huld
så älska frihet mer än guld
ty frihet följer ära.

"Freedom is the best of things..." The first line of this medieval poem and song conveys the essence of an early Swedish liberation movement. Written by Bishop Thomas of Strängnäs (1380-1443), it helped inspire the series of revolts against foreign rulers and their henchmen that led to the convening of Sweden's first Parliament in 1435.

Throughout history, there have always been — and always will be — situations where freedom is threatened or suppressed. For many Swedes and people from other countries around the world, the search for freedom led to America. Over the generations, America has continuously been rediscovered by new groups from many lands, who arrive in search of liberty and opportunity.

Let us listen to the grandson of one couple who, like thousands of others, left their Swedish homeland in the mid-19th century and began life afresh in a new country. His name was Carl Sandburg (1878-1967), and he wrote this poem in 1950:

Freedom is a habit
and a coat worn
some born to wear it
some never to know it.
Freedom is cheap
or again as a garment
is so costly
men pay their lives
rather than not have it.

Most of those who find their way to America have one thing in common: they all want to know freedom. This may be a highly tangible freedom from hunger, poverty and repression. Or it may be an emotional freedom: lifting an invisible yoke from the shoulders. Freedom of thought, the banishing of old "musts," the opening of new dimensions beyond the reality that they thought at first was the whole world.

All those who have the privilege of experiencing freedom in its various guises and dimensions share a strong awareness of the individual accountability that goes with it. To those who are truly mature, freedom also means shouldering responsibilities.

That is America to me.

Göran Blomé

Carl Milles' sculpture,
"Man and His Genius"

A New World unfolds to every visitor, as it did to those who arrived from Asia across a spit of land in the far northwest, to the Norsemen who came by sea from the northeast and to all the others who sailed there across warmer, more southerly waters.

North America, once the world's last great wilderness, is now a melting pot for people from every continent, a platform for mankind's onward journey from earth into outer space.

This remarkable bit of our planet has rich fertile soils and inhospitable badlands, endless plains and thick forests, frozen tundras and searing deserts. It is a place of contrasts and opportunities.

Hundreds of Indian nations once ruled the territory that now makes up the fifty United States and the provinces and territories of Canada. And even today, many of the natural and cultural features of North America transcend its artificial political boundaries.

It is a continent with the world's largest industrial belt, stretching from New York and Philadelphia to the western shores of Lake Michigan, hugging Lake Huron and bumping into Quebec – which is culturally speaking a country all its own, as is the region stretching from Boston across the border and north to Newfoundland. The South was briefly a country all its own, and in many ways remains one –from Washington D.C. south to the Florida keys and west to the Rio Grande, where it blends into the cultures of the Caribbean and Latin America.

In the middle of the continent are the Great Plains, fenced in to the west by mountain chains that stretch all the way north to Alaska. Beyond their summits, the turbulent Pacific coast forms a barrier to those who have continued pushing west. Once there, they can travel no further by land, and those who have not found all the freedoms they have sought can explore the inner landscape. So the Far West has become a land of dream factories, a global center of rapidly changing technologies built on human intelligence and imagination.

This book examines the opportunities North America has provided – and continues to provide – to individuals and businesses with a Swedish or Swedish-American background. It focuses largely on entrepreneurs who have sought greater freedom and tried to fulfill their dreams of a happier life. It is a small slice of Swedish-American reality and an even smaller slice of the North American dynamic.

Newfoundland

Halifax

In the wake of the Vikings

Three major companies embody Sweden's corporate soul perhaps better than any others:
1) Stora, the world's oldest industrial corporation, today one of the world's largest forest product groups, a national crown jewel that is now part of the Wallenberg family sphere.
2) Volvo, which sprang from 20th century technology and entrepreneurial energy, a group that has always sought to be independent of any major shareholders.
3) IKEA, created after World War II by a single entrepreneur, Ingvar Kamprad, whose ethical and economic sensibility, and humility toward customers, have become the guiding principles of his company.

All three companies know how to take proper advantage of nature's resources and laws. This is the only way a company can survive in the long run. So it seems quite logical that they followed in the wake of the Vikings, by building their first North American production bases near the continent's closest ice-free harbors to Sweden: in Nova Scotia.

Bodies and major components like engines, transmissions, wiring systems and seats arrive in crates and are assembled at two identical marriage point stations operated in tandem.

First European auto assembly plant in post-war North America

Volvo was regarded as daring when it became the first European automobile manufacturer to establish an assembly operation in North America after World War II. The year was 1963, and this was also Volvo's first overseas assembly plant. The company had a clear strategy: to turn North America into its second "domestic" market. This bold, forward-looking move was actually a virtue born of a necessity: to overcome then-existing tariff barriers. During the plant's first year of operations, 1,139 series 122 Volvos were assembled. By 1966 production had reached 3,701 cars. The following year, Volvo moved to a larger factory in Halifax. By the mid-1980s it was obvious that a newer facility was needed to accommodate the new P70 model. So Volvo built its third plant and moved again. Today Volvo is a major employer in the Halifax area, proud of its winning combination of Swedish technology and Canadian craftsmanship. The model that dominates assembly today is the 850 series. At the Halifax plant, cars receive the loving care that is required to ensure high quality. (Don't tell anybody, but the cars assembled in Halifax have achieved the top quality ranking among Volvo's auto assembly plants.)

Both finished cars and semi-knocked down (SKD) kits for assembly are shipped on a continuous basis from Europe to Halifax, Volvo's gateway to the Canadian and northeastern U.S. markets.

Volvo's third plant in Halifax is a model facility, both in terms of technology and working methods.

Vice President and General Manager Kaj Nielsen focuses on achieving quality through a teamwork philosophy.

Each section of the assembly line is organized into a team, and individual operators have broad responsibilities in the assembly process. Suggesting and implementing improvements is a natural element of their job.

The causeway – a bridge to Sweden

In 1955 the completion of the Canso Causeway, at 200 feet the world's deepest structure of its kind, forced the closure of the main local industry, a ferry service between mainland Nova Scotia and Cape Breton Island. At the same time the causeway created an ice-free harbor along the Strait of Canso, a natural channel connecting the Gulf of St. Lawrence with the Atlantic Ocean. With it came opportunities for industrial development.

All available resources were pressed into the task of luring new industries to the Strait area. An abundance of natural resources, particularly sizable timberlands in northeastern Nova Scotia and Cape Breton, were a selling point when local officials approached the world's oldest industrial corporation, Sweden's Stora Kopparberg, which was founded in the late 13th century. These contacts led to the creation of what is now Stora Forest Industries, located near the small town of Port Hawkesbury. The Nova Scotia government granted the company a forest management license for all Crown lands in the province's seven eastern counties. Stora set up its woodlands operation in the late 1950s and officially started up its market pulp mill in January 1962.

For Stora, opening a mill on Cape Breton Island made good sense. From there, it could ship products both south to the United States

and east to Europe. So the Causeway had also opened a commercial "bridge" over the Atlantic that followed an old Viking route all the way back to Scandinavia.

In 1971 Stora expanded and broadened the facility to include a large newsprint mill. Late in 1995 the company approved an investment of C$650 million to build an uncoated magazine paper machine to supply this value-added product to North American and world markets. In the same year, it completed a C$48 million secondary treatment system to clean its process water.

Stora's commitment to forest renewal is manifested in its efforts on behalf of the massive regeneration of Cape Breton Island's Crown land forests, which were devastated by the spruce budworm in the 1970s. And in 1995 its long-term program to regrow more trees than it harvests from the company's managed forest lands marked a milestone when the 100 millionth seedling was planted at its Queensville tract, not far from the Canso Causeway.

In March 1996, Nova Scotia Lieutenant Governor John James Kinley told the opening session of the provincial General Assembly: "Stora has become a model corporate citizen in our region."

IKEA's first bridgehead

Halifax, Nova Scotia was IKEA's first bridge-head on the western shore of the Atlantic — in two senses. When the Swedish-owned home furnishings chain was preparing its North American market debut during the mid-1970s, it chose Halifax, the closest ice-free port to Europe, as the site of its first superstore. The company has always based its expansion strategy on carefully thought-out logistic planning, with one store often serving as a platform for launching the next one. This also happened in Halifax; new stores followed elsewhere in Canada. The Halifax store itself had to be closed after a few years, because the market there turned out to be too small. But having launched its offensive in North America, soon IKEA realized it would also need manufacturing capacity there. Soon production was in full swing at Swedwood Canada, an IKEA-affiliated company up in the hills of Dartmouth, north of Halifax harbor. Behind a modest facade is one of the world's most modern factories for processing board into flat furniture assembly kits. Plant Manager Tommy Holmer (right) leads a team of about 150 highly motivated employees who produce and ship Billy bookshelves, Kurs dressers and other IKEA top sellers to the chain's stores in Canada and the United States.

Innovator on the North Atlantic

Ships bearing the three giant letters ACL can be spotted every week in the harbors of Halifax, New York, Baltimore and Portsmouth in North America. They arrive on fixed days and at fixed times with cargoes from Gothenburg, Antwerp, Liverpool, Bremerhaven and other European ports. They are the world's largest combination Roll-On/Roll-Off container ships and are specially designed for North Atlantic shipments of containers, RoRo cargoes, cars and other vehicles. The company they sail for, Atlantic Container Line, is something as unusual as a Swedish-registered corporation with its world headquarters in the United States: South Plainfield, New Jersey, to be exact.

Today ACL is a publicly held company listed on the Oslo Stock Exchange, but it all began in 1967 as a joint venture between British, French, Dutch and three Swedish shipowners. The first headquarters were in Stockholm, but later moved to Southampton, England, then to

New Jersey, where the management tackled the job of further modernizing and streamlining a shipping line that was a pioneer not only in terms of its vessels and cargo technology, but also data technology, documentation, satellite communications, equipment interchangeability and more.

The company is kept together by a single information system linking every office and local salesperson on both sides of the Atlantic. This is how the company has taken command of prices, schedules, cargo flows, import-export balances and a comprehensive distribution service that includes ACL's inland transportation system, with offices and depots throughout the Eastern and Midwestern states. Its management and employees are committed to exploring innovative ways to make it even easier to do business with ACL.

You can almost set your watch by the arrival of ACL's vessels at their regular ports, here Port Elizabeth, New Jersey.

Two Swedes stationed at a Swedish-registered company with its headquarters in New Jersey: Bernhard Ryding, President (right) and his colleague Nils Erikson, Information Officer.

The American dream

Sweden's first dream of America was the colonizing vision of a European Great Power. This dream came true one March day in 1638, when two ships – the Kalmar Nyckel and Fogel Grip – sailed up the Delaware River to establish the colony of New Sweden.

Sweden had been conquering new territory around the Baltic since the Middle Ages and became a genuine Great Power under King Gustav II Adolf, who died in the Thirty Years' War in 1632. Now his ambitious Chancellor, Axel Oxenstierna, who had been appointed to rule Sweden until the future Queen Christina came of age, wanted to establish a trans-Atlantic colony. The leader of the partially Dutch-financed Swedish expedition to the Delaware River region was Peter Minuit, former governor of New Netherland (later New York).

The two vessels anchored on the river and a party was dispatched to shore, purchasing land from five Indian chiefs. The Swedes built a mili-

tary post, Fort Christina, on the site of present-day Wilmington, Delaware. This marked the beginning of a 17-year period when large tracts on both sides of the Delaware River, including present-day Philadelphia, became Swedish territory. But in September 1655 the colony's governor capitulated at Fort Christina to superior Dutch forces commanded by New Netherland Governor Peter Stuyvesant. Sweden's American colonial dream came to an abrupt end.

The New Sweden epoch may have been brief, but it signified the beginning of a very close relationship between Sweden and what later became the United States of America. The inhabitants of a small, thinly populated country on the northern periphery of Europe were thus among the earliest European immigrants in the new land. Only the British, Spaniards, French-

The arrival of the Swedes in Delaware on the Kalmar Nyckel, as portrayed in a 1928 ceiling painting by artist Christian von Schneidau in the lobby of the American Swedish Historical Museum in Philadelphia.

Nineteenth century Swedish emigrants make their way across the Atlantic in a scene from the new musical Kristina from Duvemåla, based on Vilhelm Moberg's emigration novels. The music is by Benny Andersson, the lyrics by Björn Ulvaeus (the two B's in ABBA).

men and Dutchmen arrived earlier. The first voyage of the Kalmar Nyckel and Fogel Grip to the Delaware River took place a mere 18 years after the Mayflower had first anchored off the Massachusetts coast.

The first businessman

Although New Sweden was a central government project – and most of the earliest colonists were administrators, soldiers and seamen – there were also entrepreneurs aboard the vessels that arrived periodically from Sweden.

Born in Västergötland province in 1621, Jonas Nilsson became perhaps the first independent Swedish businessman in America. He arrived in New Sweden in 1643 to serve as a soldier at Fort Elfsborg, located on what is now the New Jersey side of the Delaware River. After the collapse of Swedish rule in 1655, he settled at Kingsessing, a trading post in an area

that is now part of Philadelphia. There he bartered European goods – mainly in exchange for pelts – with the local Indians.

Jonas Nilsson, who died in 1693, was followed by many other successful Swedish immigrants who started doing business and built up companies. But the economy of Colonial America was highly regulated and did not yet offer the entrepreneurial opportunities that the United States would later provide.

Not until the large 19th century waves of immigration would the Swedes become a significant factor in American business. During their Great Power period of the 17th and early 18th centuries, and for many decades afterward, very few of them were interested in emigrating. But New Sweden served as an early platform in America. Meanwhile a few Swedes were arriving in other colonies such as New York and Massachusetts during the 17th century.

As early as 1639, a sea captain named Jonas Bronck (or Brunk), born on a farm in the Swedish province of Småland, arrived via Holland at New Netherland. He was the first immigrant

Next to the Christina River in Wilmington, Delaware, a private entrepreneur is building a replica of the Kalmar Nyckel.

Holy Trinity (Old Swedes Church), Wilmington, erected in 1698-99, is the oldest sanctuary in the U.S. continuing to hold regular services.

to settle in what later became the New York City borough of The Bronx.

In 1642 peace negotiations between the Dutch colonists and the previous Indian owners of the land were held at Jonas Bronck's home, just across the water from Manhattan. In memory of the resulting peace treaty, The Bronx was named for him – with only a slight change of spelling.

Meanwhile other Swedish immigrants and their descendants began to leave their mark in American history. John Morton of Pennsylvania cast the decisive vote when the Declaration of Independence was adopted by the Continental Congress. Another descendent of New Sweden settlers was John Hanson of Maryland, President of the Continental Congress during the first year after the American revolution (1781-82).

Even before the beginning of large-scale Swedish emigration, close ties and potential business opportunities between the new United States and Sweden were manifested in the 1783 Treaty of Amity and Commerce signed by Benjamin Franklin and Swedish ambassador Gustav Philip Creutz. It was the first such treaty that the United States signed (except for one with its military ally, France) after making peace with Great Britain. The treaty is still in force today.

Today Bishop Hill is a heavily visited state historical site, with many of the original buildings from the Jansonist period still preserved, for example the Colony Hotel shown here. In 1996 Swedish-Americans celebrated the 150th anniversary of the Bishop Hill settlement with a nationwide Immigration Jubilee including hundreds of cultural events and a royal visit from Sweden.

Large-scale organized Swedish immigration to the United States began only in the 1840s, when a group known as the Jansonists – who were fleeing religious intolerance in their homeland – settled in Bishop Hill, Illinois under the leadership of the charismatic Pastor Erik Jansson.

They were followed by thousands of other Swedes. Many were seeking religious and political freedom, while others were mainly fleeing poverty and hoping to find better economic opportunities in the New World. Despite ups and downs, the flow of Swedish emigrants con-

Immigrant implements and an early character reference, The Swedish American Museum Center, Chicago, Illinois.

tinued for more than 70 years. The peak occurred in 1887, when 37,000 Swedes arrived in the United States. For a time, Sweden was contributing more immigrants to the United States per capita than any other nation except Ireland. During the 70 biggest years of emigration, Sweden lost about one fourth of its population to America.

The wave of Swedish immigration subsided in the 1920s, and the 1930 census revealed that 1,562,703 U.S. inhabitants had either been born in Sweden or in America of Swedish parents.

By way of Ellis Island

Most Swedes stepped ashore at Ellis Island in New York harbor, and early in the 20th century, New York was the city with the largest concentration of Swedes in the United States after Chicago.

Many of those who settled in New York were skilled craftsmen or engaged in commerce and shipping. They tended to be well-educated and materially well off. A fair number were adventurers of one kind or another.

One of the best-known Swedish immigrants in New York was the Värmland-born engineer and inventor John Ericsson, who arrived in New York in 1839 at the age of 36. He performed a number of engineering assignments for the U.S. Navy and went on to design the armored vessel Monitor, which played a key role in the Civil War sea battle against the Confederate ironclad Merrimac. From 1864 until his death in 1889, Ericsson lived on Beach Street in Manhattan.

Sven (or Svante) Magnus Swenson, one of the best-known early Swedish businessmen in America, began his career in the cotton trade in Texas during the late 1830s, while it was still an independent country. He became a wealthy merchant, bought land near the capital of Austin, settled there and attracted many other Swedish settlers. Because his sympathies lay

With a model of the Monitor in one hand and the blueprints for it in the other, John Ericsson has been standing watch in Battery Park, near his long-time Manhattan home, since 1903.

Kenneth Sjogren is responsible for a large part of Lindsborg's production of Dala horses, having painted well over 20,000 of these folk art objects, which originated in Dalarna (Dalecarlia) province.

with the Union side during the Civil War, he was forced to flee briefly to Mexico. After the war he became a cotton exporter in New Orleans, but he soon moved to New York and established a Wall Street banking firm later known as S.M. Swenson & Sons. He continued to function as a link to Swedish business interests in Texas. In 1896 he died in Brooklyn, a multimillionaire.

One of his sons was Eric P. Swenson, also a successful banker. In the 1920s he served as chairman of National City Bank, which later became part of America's largest bank, Citicorp.

Go west!

Many immigrants from Sweden were farmers who had been plagued by bad harvests and poor living conditions in their homeland. As a rule, they hardly paused in New York once they had made it through Ellis Island, but continued directly to the Midwest in search of land. Even after the industrialization of America intensified and large numbers of people began moving into the major cities, the stream of Swedish immigrants continued to flow in the opposite direction.

To rural Swedes, land ownership was still the self-evident path toward greater prosperity

and social prestige. By the late 19th century, however, most of the fertile farmland in the central Midwest had already been taken by other immigrant groups who had arrived there first. Lively property speculation was making it harder for the often impecunious Swedes to buy land in the central Midwest, so they continued north from their temporary stopping place in Chicago.

The relatively unpopulated expanses of Minnesota, Wisconsin and the Dakotas became the new home of many Swedes. Other settlers, including stubborn Yankees, had been there earlier but had given up. Some Swedish immigrants continued north all the way into Canada, and a large group settled in Winnipeg. Swedish farmers were accustomed to a severe climate and inhospitable growing conditions; many of those who put down roots on the northern prairies were successful, and they created new prosperity for their children and subsequent generations.

Dala horses in Kansas

One very important factor in determining where the emigrants chose to settle was how well each place marketed itself back home in Sweden. The last of the Swedish religious settlements in the United States was Lindsborg,

The Dala horse, the symbol of Lindsborg, even decorates its post office.

By the 1890s, many Swedes in Chicago had moved into the area surrounding Clark and Foster Avenues, which became known as Andersonville.

located in the Smoky River Valley of Kansas. Swedes began arriving there in the 1860s, and in 1879 an energetic Swedish-American, the Rev. Carl Aaron Swensson (1857-1904), took over as pastor of the local Swedish congregation at Bethany Lutheran Church. In 1881 he founded Bethany College. Lindsborg and the college received so much favorable press coverage in Sweden that, according to legend, one immigrant arriving in New York burst out: "If this is New York, what must Lindsborg be!" Today Lindsborg, symbolized by a Dala horse, is one of the most lively centers of Swedish culture in the United States.

An oasis for those who crave Swedish food.

According to the 1930 census, 900,000 Swedes – well over half those living in the United States – resided in the twelve Midwestern states of Ohio, Indiana, Illinois, Michigan, Wisconsin, Minnesota, Iowa, Missouri, North Dakota, South Dakota, Nebraska and Kansas.

Nowhere was Swedish influence as clear as in Minnesota. In 1930 more than 10 percent of that state's population consisted of Swedes. By then, many had long since left their farms,

moved into cities and taken industrial jobs. Those who had arrived in the United States after the turn of the century generally settled in the cities from the beginning. For one large group, the vibrant and rapidly expanding industrial center of Chicago was the right place to be.

Swedish cities

As early as 1900, there were 144,719 Swedish residents of Chicago. Meanwhile the second largest city in Sweden itself, Gothenburg, had a population of only 130,619. In other words, the second largest Swedish city in the world was Chicago.

Swedish immigrants soon built a reputation as capable craftsmen and independent workers, especially in the rapidly growing construction industry. It was a common saying that the wooden city of Chicago was hammered together with Swedish nails by Swedish carpenters. Many immigrants from Sweden also helped build the skyscrapers that began rising in Chicago and New York early in the 20th century.

Numerous Swedes took the opportunity to get ahead as entrepreneurs and business own-

ers. Some built companies based on their own inventions or those of others., or used their expertise as craftsmen to start furniture or iron-working plants. In the Chicago area, the Swedes became especially well known as skilled tool makers and owners of mechanical workshops.

Other leading Swedish-American manufacturing centers were Jamestown, New York; Rockford, Illinois; and Grand Rapids, Michigan.

In Jamestown, Charles P. Dahlström, who had arrived in the United States in 1890, started the Dahlstrom Metallic Door Company in 1904. Its main product – a fireproof metal door – was his own invention. Sold on a large scale throughout the U.S., it was considered especially suitable for new skyscrapers. For example, the company delivered 50,000 doors to Rockefeller Center, the largest planned commercial complex in Midtown Manhattan, which was built during the Depression years of the 1930s.

In Chicago, Värmland-born Charles S. Peterson started to work in the printing trade after arriving in 1887 at the age of 14. Twelve years later he started the Peterson Linotyping Company, which eventually became the largest printing group in the United States. As a city official in the 1920s, he was among the prime movers behind the success of the 1933 Chicago world's fair.

Vincent Bendix (1881-1945), who came from Småland, founded Bendix Aviation, a major supplier to the aviation and defense

The Swedes brought with them to America the art of building log cabins, including this large version which houses the Marionette Theater in New York City's Central Park.

industry. Stockholm-born Alfred Stromberg and Östergötland-born Androv Carlson were pioneering telephone manufacturers in America. Their company, Stromberg-Carlson, is now part of the Siemens group. A Swedish-American named George William Borg founded a clutch manufacturing company that was among the forerunners of Borg-Warner, a major industrial group he later headed.

Meanwhile thousands of Swedes sought work in the flourishing automotive industry of Michigan. In 1901 Charles Blomström, who had emigrated from Småland with his parents, started the Blomstrom Motor Car Company. One of the largest automobile plants in Detroit, it produced 30-40 cars a week. Later he formed a company that made a large car called the Blomstrom, but this make soon disappeared in the tough competitive climate of the early automotive industry.

Like the Blomstrom automobile, many companies founded by Swedes vanished as a result of the massive restructuring that American business has undergone throughout the 20th century.

But many of their names survive, and some are household names in America today. Charles Walgreen (1873-1939), born in Illinois of Swedish parents, began working in a shoe factory in Dixon, but injured his hand and instead took a job at a drugstore. Soon he bought the store, then continued to expand his business. It grew into a chain of several hundred. Today there are 2,100 Walgreens drug stores in more than 30 states and the company's annual sales are in excess of $10 billion.

Greyhound

Carl Eric Wickman, born in Dalarna (Dalecarlia) province in 1887, arrived in the United States at age 17 and worked at a lumber mill in Arizona. Moving from there to Hibbing, Minnesota, he took a job in a mine and soon discovered that the workers needed daily transportation from their homes to the mines and home again. So he bought a used seven-seat Hupmobile and began a small-scale commuter service. His venture was so successful that he was soon able to buy buses and form the company that eventually grew into Greyhound Lines. By 1934 Wickman was President and proprietor of an enterprise that owned 1,900 buses and controlled many more in a network of scheduled bus services stretching from coast to coast. Since then, generations of Americans have crossed the continent on Greyhound buses. The company still serves 2,400 destinations today, although competition from low-cost airline flights has become more difficult in recent years.

The original Walgreens (1901) on Chicago's South Side, seen here, grew into the leading drug store chain in the United States.

The farm in northern Sweden that was John Nordström's 1871 birthplace was taken over, as custom dictated, by his older brother. Being the second son, John had to seek his fortune elsewhere. In Seattle, the family business that he founded nearly a century ago is still growing and has plenty of room for several Nordstrom sons at a time. Below: The Nordstrom store in downtown Seattle.

The first and second generations. John W. Nordstrom (seated) with his sons Elmer, Everett and Lloyd Nordstrom.

The third generation management team. Jack McMillan (husband of Lloyd Nordstrom's daughter Loyal), Bruce Nordstrom, Bob Bender (a friend since childhood), John Nordstrom and Jim Nordstrom.

The fourth generation taking charge. Dan, Jim A., Bill, Blake, Erik and Pete Nordstrom.

Nordstrom

Another Swedish immigrant saga began in 1887 when 16-year-old country boy John Nordström arrived in New York with $5 in his pocket and without knowing English. He worked his way across the continent to California, then north to Washington, which was attracting many Swedes because the lumber industry and the paper mills there needed labor. But Nordstrom continued to Alaska and to the Klondike region of northern Canada to prospect for gold. While his efforts did not make him fabulously rich, he returned to Seattle with $13,000 and became co-owner of a shoe store operated by another Swede, Carl Wallin.

Their well-regarded and profitable shoe business in Seattle was eventually taken over by John Nordstrom's three sons Everett, Elmer and Lloyd, who diversified it into men's and women's clothing and expanded it along the west coast. Today Nordstrom is one of the largest, most successful fashion chains in the United States, with specialty stores in 14 states. Since 1968 the company has been run by the third generation of Nordstroms, and in recent years they have gradually brought the fourth generation into the management team. Although the retail chain is a listed company with revenues of more than $4 billion a year, it is still controlled by the Nordstrom family.

Advertising men

Alfred Erickson, born in New York state in 1876 of Swedish parents, was among the pioneers of modern American advertising. He started an agency under his own name, later merging it with a competitor to form McCann-Erickson. For decades, the company has created marketing and corporate image campaigns for clients like Coca-Cola. Today it is among the world's largest and most internationalized producers of advertising.

During 1995 McCann-Erickson acquired Anderson & Lembke – an agency internationally known for its business-to-business and computer industry advertising – from its Swedish-born, U.S.-based executives, Hans Ullmark and Steve Trygg, who remain at its helm.

Co-founder of Texas Instruments

Erik Jonsson (1901-1995) was born in Brooklyn, New York and grew up on Bedford Avenue

Erik Jonsson (1901-1995) was born in Brooklyn, New York of Swedish parents, co-founded Texas Instruments Inc. and served as Mayor of Dallas in 1964-71.

with his Swedish immigrant parents. Later in life, he moved to Dallas and was one of the three men who founded Texas Instruments, a multinational electronics giant. He eventually also became the mayor of Dallas.

In his capacity as chairman of the Southwest Center for Advanced Studies and President of the Dallas Citizens Council, Erik Jonsson, accompanied by his wife Margaret, joined Dallas Mayor Earle Cabell at Love Field on November 22, 1963. There they met Air Force One when it arrived after a brief flight from nearby Fort Worth. On board were President and Mrs. John F. Kennedy, Vice President and Mrs. Lyndon Johnson and Governor and Mrs. John Connally. The Kennedys, Johnsons, Connallys and Cabells assembled for a motorcade through downtown Dallas.

Meanwhile Erik Jonsson and his wife headed directly to the Dallas Trade Mart, where he would be the official host at a luncheon, where the president was scheduled to address 2,600 invited guests. But as we know, Kennedy was assassinated on the way to the Trade Mart.

The calmness and determination with which Erik Jonsson helped deal with the tumult that broke out in Dallas that day made him a self-evident candidate for mayor the following year. Dallas needed a man who could infuse a new spirit in the city after the wave of grief and sense of guilt that had followed the Kennedy assassination. Jonsson served as Mayor from 1964 to 1971.

Leading business executives

Many other Swedish-Americans have reached leading positions in major American corporations. At General Motors, for example, Oscar Lundin served as Executive Vice President for finance, and the brothers Peter and William Hoglund are both former Vice Presidents of GM. Their grandfather emigrated from Sweden to the American Midwest around 1890. Their father, Elis Hoglund, applied for a job at General Motors and – because he spoke Swedish – was sent to GM in Denmark and later in Stockholm. He advanced to a top position at Opel in Germany, but when World War II broke out the family moved back to the United States.

Another "GM Swede" is Elmer W. Johnson, who held various offices at GM in the 1980s. When he resumed his law practice as a partner at the firm of Kirkland & Ellis in 1988, he was a member of the executive and finance committees of the GM board. Johnson, born in Denver in 1932, has also worked with the

Elmer W. Johnson, born in Denver, Colorado, is a highly respected figure in the Swedish-American community, though he keeps a low profile. In addition to his careers at General Motors and as a partner of the Chicago-based law firm of Kirkland & Ellis, he is a trustee and executive committee member of the Aspen Institute USA, where he occasionally serves as a seminar moderator. A Fellow of the American Academy of Arts and Sciences and member of its Midwest Council, he has written many articles on ethical issues related to business, the legal profession and public policy.

Rudolph (Rudy) Peterson was born in Svenljunga, Sweden in 1904. When he was an infant, the family was visited by his maternal aunt and uncle from America, who offered to bring his then 3-year-old sister to America. Instead they were allowed to give one-year-old Rudolph a new home in America and to adopt him.

Rudy Peterson lived in Youngstown, Ohio and in Los Angeles, then grew up outside Turlock in California's Central Valley. Working his way up in the finance and banking world, he served from 1963-70 as President and CEO at Bank of America, where he still maintains an office. He was Swedish American of the Year in 1965 and won the Great Swedish Heritage Award in 1996.

Sundstrand Corporation in Rockford, Illinois, which was named for David Sundstrand, one of the many technically gifted Swedish-American entrepreneurs in that city. In 1914 he designed a 10-key adding machine. Today Sundstrand Corporation is a $1.6 billion, Fortune 500 company with 9,200 employees worldwide that manufactures electronics for aerospace contractors.

The golden state

However, the state that has attracted the largest number of Swedes is neither Minnesota nor Illinois, but California. They began moving there in large numbers during the 1870s, though gold seekers, sailors and traders had arrived as early as the 1840s. A Swedish-Norwegian consulate (the two countries formed a union at the time) was established in 1850 in San Francisco, which together with Los Angeles attracted

about 40 percent of the state's Swedish immigrants. Otherwise many of their compatriots put down roots in the San Joaquin Valley, with Kingsburg and Turlock as the two most important Swedish settlements.

Among the Swedish farmers who moved to California's Central Valley were the parents of Roy Anderson, who was born in Ripon in 1920. In 1977 he was appointed Chairman of Lockheed, one of America's biggest defense contractors. His task was to save the company after one of the most highly publicized corporate scandals in American business history.

Frederick O'Green, born in 1921 in Mason City, Iowa of a Swedish father and a Finnish mother, also worked at Lockheed, leaving a position as technical director of its space programs to join Litton Industries, another California-based military equipment maker, where he became Chairman in 1981. (O'Green, which

A powerful Swedish-American landmark: The twin 699-foot towers of Atlantic Richfield and the Bank of America, built by close friends Robert O. Andersson and Rudolph Peterson.

otherwise sounds Irish, was an Americanization of the Swedish name Ågren.)

Two very visible Swedish-American landmarks in downtown Los Angeles are the twin 52-story towers of Atlantic Richfield Plaza and the Bank of America, the result of a handshake between two close friends. One was Robert O. Anderson (born 1917 in Chicago, son of the legendary banker Hugo Anderson, who emigrated from Helsingborg, Sweden). For more than 20 years during the 1960s, 70s and 80s he was a major shareholder and Chairman of ARCO. The other was Rudolph A. Peterson, who was born in Sweden in 1904 but grew up in Turlock. Between 1963 and 1970 he was President and CEO of Bank of America.

The Swedish king of Minnesota

The man who perhaps best personifies the successful Swedish-American is Curtis L. Carlson, whose grandparents emigrated from Småland and Värmland provinces in the 19th century and settled in Minnesota. Born in 1914 in Minneapolis, he began learning about business from his father, who opened his own grocery store when Curt was a little boy. Curt developed his business acumen as a caddy, newspaper boy and Procter & Gamble soap salesman. While still holding the latter job, he began to sell trading stamps to mom and pop grocery stores around Minneapolis. With $55 in borrowed funds, he established the Gold Bond Stamp Company. At first the business grew slowly, but by the late 1960s it had gone international. Meanwhile the trading stamp vogue had peaked, and Curtis Carlson began to diversify into new businesses.

Today he owns one of America's largest privately held corporations, Carlson Companies, with annual systemwide revenues of more than $11.6 billion. It includes one of the world's two largest travel agency businesses, the Carlson Travel Group, of which Carlson Wagonlit Travel is a part. It also includes Carlson Hospitality Worldwide with its Radisson and Country Inn & Suites By Carlson hotel chains as well as the T.G.I. Friday's, Country Kitchen, Italianni's and Front Row Sports Grill restaurant chains. The corporation's other business is Carlson Marketing Group, an international company that helps businesses improve their sales and/or profits through motivation, loyalty and event marketing solutions.

Carlson's original product, Gold Bond stamps, has entered a new, high-tech phase and is called Gold Points Plus. This new electronic marketing program, found in grocery and other retail stores, is enjoying a most successful run as a loyalty program in today's marketplace.

Despite the size of his corporate empire, Carlson has retained the company's "family business" character. His daughter, Marilyn Carlson Nelson, has assumed an increasing share of his executive duties, and Marilyn's son, Curtis Carlson Nelson, has also joined the group's management team.

Over the years, Curtis Carlson and his family have maintained strong and frequent contact with the "old country." In recent years, his company has also begun to invest in Sweden. For example, it has established a partnership with Scandinavian Airlines to operate the Radisson SAS hotel chain in Europe. Another milestone occurred in 1996 when Sweden's first T.G.I. Friday's restaurant opened on Stureplan in central Stockholm.

The pendulum thus seems to be swinging back from the New World to the Old, as Curtis Carlson's blend of Swedish cultural heritage and American entrepreneurial energy begins to make its influence felt back in Sweden.

Another dream coming true: The Curtis L. Carlson School of Management's new building at the University of Minnesota in Minneapolis is scheduled to open in late 1997. Curt Carlson, for whom the school was renamed in 1986, is the largest private benefactor of this $45 million project and over the years has contributed and helped raise more than $375 million for the university which is his alma mater.

World without limits

In 1961 Curtis L. Carlson, assisted by super-salesman Sandy Saver — symbol of Gold Bond Stamps — broke ground for the first world headquarters of Carlson Companies (inset below left), having just bought 1,000 acres of farmland west of Minneapolis. Little did he suspect back then how many equally important milestones would follow in his incredible entrepreneurial career. Some 30 years later, he built another world headquarters (left) in the same area. "Not trying to make it big at once" is one of his mottos. After starting his career as a newspaper boy and a soap salesman, he has methodically built up one of America's largest closely held companies. Visitors entering Carlson's spectacular twin tower headquarters can pause to contemplate Carl Milles' tour de force of sculptural flight, "Man and His Genius," a high-spirited, unrestrained work that exults in life and inspires mankind to envision a world without limits.

Curtis L. Carlson, his daughter Marilyn Carlson Nelson and her son Curtis Carlson Nelson in the Viking Revival Room, with original panels and furniture created at the turn of the century by Norwegian carver and designer Gerhard Munthe. This alcove, located off the main entrance to Carlson Towers, is part of the executive dining room, The Retreat. The room was removed from a mansion north of Stockholm, Sweden, brought to Chicago by a famous museum and exhibited there for eight months. Carlson purchased the room, and it is now displayed in his new office building. On the back wall is a magnificent Carl Larsson painting entitled "Esbjörn the Thinker," featuring the son of this famed Swedish artist.

A glimpse of Carlson Companies

Country Inns & Suites By Carlson, the Group's newest lodging operation, is aimed at both families and the business traveler.

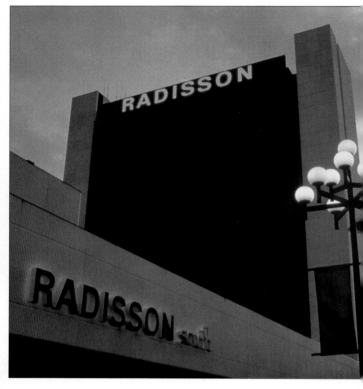

One of the first hotels built by Carlson Companies was the Radisson Hotel South & Plaza Tower in Bloomington, Minnesota, a Minneapolis suburb.

T.G.I. Friday's guests have made it America's number one specialty restaurant company, with the highest per-unit sales volume of any international chain.

Carlson Marketing Group offers incentive travel planning, consumer loyalty management, database marketing and other promotions services.

Carlson Wagonlit Travel reserves more airline seats than any other company in the world, making it the largest single customer of many airlines. The SAS Hotels division of Scandinavian Airlines System also operates Radisson SAS Hotel chain in Europe and the Middle East as part of Radisson Hotels Worldwide.

The luxurious twin hulled 350-passenger SSC Radisson Diamond is part of the fleet of Radisson Seven Seas cruises.

Carlson Wagonlit Travel, one of the two largest travel management companies in the world, was formed in 1994 through the union of Minneapolis-based Carlson Travel Network and Paris-based Wagonlit Travel, a descendant of the originators of the Orient Express. Carlson Travel Network is the descendant of the oldest U.S. travel agency chain, Ask Mr. Foster, founded in 1888 by Ward G. Foster in St. Augustine, Florida. All Carlson Travel Network agencies will convert to the Carlson Wagonlit Travel brand name by January 1997.

Reason to be proud

Ulla and Bertil Brunk and their son Lars have reason to be proud. Despite many difficulties, they have worked hard and fulfilled their dream. Ulla and Bertil belong to the post-war Swedish emigrant generation. Ulla came to Chicago with her parents in 1949. In 1952 Bertil, then a 25-year-old master tool and die maker, visited a relative in Danbury, Connecticut and then continued to Chicago, the center of opportunity for tool and die professionals in the Midwest.

The couple met at a dance held by a Chicago-area Swedish organization. They traveled to Sweden and got married in Stockholm during the fall of 1954, but after only a few months they decided to move back to the U.S. And that is where they have stayed.

After holding several jobs in his specialty, Bertil established his own small tool and die company in 1960 in Lake Geneva, Wisconsin, with Ulla as his partner. Bertil's responsibilities were managing the tool room and the designing of dies, while Ulla's responsibilities focused on running day-to-day company operations. In 1970 Brunk Tool & Die purchased its first punch press. This was the start of the highly sophisticated manufacturing facility it has grown to be. Their son Lars, who has been an integral part of the business since 1980, holds an Industrial Management degree from the University of Wyoming and has worked in all facets of the operation from early on. Their technical, managerial and business insights combined with their determination to manufacture the highest quality products have been the key to the success of what is now called Brunk Industries Inc.

Today Brunk Industries employs about 200 people and specializes in medium and high volume high-precision metal stampings and assemblies. The company's continuous dedication to excellence has been recognized by both the industry and its customers, among them Ericsson, Motorola, Johnson & Johnson, IBM, OMC, Mercury Marine and AMP. And in June 1996, Bertil Brunk, President, and Ulla Brunk, CFO, won the annual Spirit of Wisconsin Entrepreneurs of the Year Award.

Bertil and Ulla's daughter Anne is a Northwestern University graduate who holds a degree in Speech. She is a television news anchor at the CBS station in Kansas City, Missouri.

So the Brunks have reason to be proud.

The Brunks take good care of their machines, almost as if they were family members. The equipment at their plant can handle conventional and high-speed stamping, assemblies and most secondary and finishing operations.

Norwegian-Swedish union on U.S. soil

For more than 90 years (1814-1905), Norway and Sweden were joined in a union headed by the King of Sweden. Today those who drive west along Belmont Avenue, one of Chicago's seemingly endless boulevards, out to the suburb of Franklin Park near O'Hare International Airport will find another kind of Norwegian-Swedish union. Its name is Overland Bolling, and its existence seems to have been ordained by the fates some time ago.

The background is this: Between the world wars, Karl Overland grew up in the Norwegian city of Sandnes, whose sister city in Sweden is called Mariestad. Meanwhile Pehr Bolling was born in Mariestad in 1919, but at age ten he moved with his siblings and parents to the Lakeview area of Chicago, then home to many Swedish immigrants. By 1942 he had married Harriet Wikstrom, a member of another Swedish family in Chicago. In 1944 he was drafted into the Army and found himself stationed on the Pacific island of Tinian in the Marianas.

In December 1945 Pehr Bolling was discharged from the service and came back to begin his career as a tool and die designer. Many Swedes and other Scandinavians in the Midwest have chosen this profession. One of the others was the above-mentioned Karl Overland, whom fate had also brought to Chicago.

Karl Overland and Pehr Bolling worked together as tool draftsmen, designers and tool and die makers at a company that had begun using modern tool presses, which stamped out small metal parts with a tolerance of thousandths of a millimeter. In 1956 they decided to start their own metal stamping business.

Today Overland Bolling is a U.S. leader in the metal stamping industry but also has numerous international clients. Its corporate headquarters and largest plant are in Franklin Park, supported by plants in Dallas, Texas; Sturgeon Bay and Milwaukee, Wisconsin; and a European bridgehead in Delemont, Switzerland.

The company is headed by their respective sons, Ken Overland and Tom Bolling, who are thus perpetuating a Norwegian-Swedish union that two immigrants established 40 years ago on U.S. soil.

Like fathers...

Pehr Bolling and Karl Overland, retired.

The production of important components for the electronic, automotive, medical industries requires very high standards of precision at the metal stamping plants of Overland Bolling. "In Pursuit of Perfection" is the company credo.

...like sons

Tom Bolling, President and CEO (as well as Swedish honorary Consul General in Illinois) and Ken Overland, Chairman of the Board.

Welcome home

To an American, "coming home" has a profound meaning. To one group of Swedes — actually on their way to Illinois — what is now Chautauqua County, New York became a home and place of refuge as long ago as the late 1840s. Robbed as they traveled west on the Erie Canal, they found themselves standing in Buffalo one August day in 1846 with only 25¢ to their name. Resuming their journey and traveling southwest, they found their promised land in Chandlers Valley, Pennsylvania, which they called Hessel Valley after the village in Småland from which several of them came. A few years later, some of them moved to nearby Jamestown. Over the next several decades they were joined by other Swedes, many of whom arrived on the Erie Railroad from New York City.

No other city in North America has as large a percentage of people of Swedish descent as Jamestown. The city also has a Swedish Consulate, with John L. Sellstrom as honorary Consul. Mr. Sellstrom's grandfather arrived from Vimmerby, Småland province, in 1868, becoming a local businessman and one of the first financial backers of Dahlstrom Metallic Door, Jamestown's first large-scale manufacturing enterprise. John L. Sellstrom himself has run his own law firm for many years.

Jamestown is situated near Lake Chautauqua, which is famous for its natural beauty and for the the Chautauqua Institution with its Victorian architecture and Athenaeum Hotel. This lakeside historic landmark remains a vibrant center of the arts, education, religion and education, especially during its nine-week summer season.

Rich social life

The calm surface of Jamestown conceals a rich and active social life, including Swedish-American clubs and lodges. The Thule Lodge of the Vasa Order is the largest branch of the organization in America, with about 1,250 members. The local Vikings lodge is likewise the largest U.S. branch of that organization, with some 2,500 members. Both lodges have their own downtown buildings. They also operate facilities on or near Lake Chautauqua for various summer activities.

Keeping family together

Durand Peterson is not only a proud grandfather (of the family shown below) but is also an enthusiastic entrepreneur and Swedish-American. He has started several successful firms, and today he runs Southern Tier Municipal & Construction Supply Co. His grandparents came from Luleå in northern Sweden. One way in which he helps preserve his Swedish heritage is as Chairman of Jamestown Community College's Scandinavian Studies Program, which includes a Scandinavian Summer Camp run in cooperation with the YMCA in Sweden.

The Peterson family greets a photographer in their Jamestown home: Valerie and Jeffrey, son Mitchell, daughters Kristine and Caroline and their dog Flicka (Swedish for "girl").

A place for all ages

Ethel Vennman, Alice Anderl and Esther Linnea Green are all of Swedish descent. As a child, when Ethel spoke English at home, her mother sometimes responded in the language of the old country: "Speak Swedish, so I can understand!" Alice remembers the Swedish bread that was always served in her childhood home (she preferred American white bread). Esther fondly recalls the excitement of the traditional Swedish Christmas morning church service. Today they all live at the ecumenical campus of Lutheran Social Services, which includes the Gustavus Adolphus Children's Home, the Lutheran Retirement Home and the Covenant Home for the Aged.

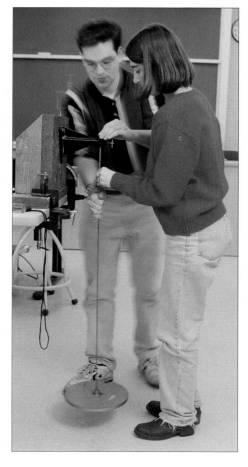

One place where young people can learn and experiment in a calm, attractive milieu is Jamestown Community College, the first such institution to be part of the State University of New York. JCC's programs are, of course, tailored to the entrepreneurial and industrial traditions of Jamestown. Its Center for Continuing Education includes a Business and Industry Center and a Small Business Development Center.

Spiritual and natural

Jamestown's First Lutheran Church is the only Swedish church in the United States designated a cathedral. The original building was constructed in 1866 by the congregation established in 1856 when the Rev. Jonas Swenson arrived from Sweden to assist the small group of immigrants who by then had settled in the town.

The Roger Tory Peterson Institute, designed by Robert A. M. Stern, honors America's pre-eminent naturalist, who was born in a Swedish-American family in Jamestown.

A door to prosperity

When David G. Dawson's paternal grandfather, Axel Gustafson, arrived in Ellis Island in 1910, he had only the mandatory $25, which his mother had sewn into his clothing. A stranger named Dawson bought his first meal in America and then helped him find his way to the Erie Railroad train that carried him west to Jamestown, New York. When Gustafson later decided to take an American name, his choice was easy. That is why the company that continues the Jamestown door and sheet metal making tradition is called Dawson Metal, not Gustafson Metal. Now managed by the third generation of the family (John, David and Jane), Dawson Metal began by making metal components for regional manufacturers like IBM but today serves an international customer base. Its Daw-son Doors division produces stainless and bronze metal doors and frames for such prestigious customers as Tiffany & Co. And need we mention what company made the door of the main entrance at the Ellis Island Museum of Immigration?

Dawson Metal's Chief Engineer and Industrial Sales Manager is a more recent Swedish immigrant, Lars E. Wallin of Särna.

Keeping traditions alive

As President of the Aarque Companies, Heidi A. Nauleau is continuing the industrial tradition represented by her father, R. Quintus Anderson, who remains Chairman. Since 1978 the Jamestown-based company has invested principally in the metal fabrication industry. Prior to establishing Aarque, Mr. Anderson was Chairman and CEO of Dahlstrom Corp. Aarque's current portfolio includes Cold Metal Products Company in Youngstown, Ohio, operating eight plants in the Unted States and Canada; Kardex Systems, formerly the Office Equipment Division of the Sperry Rand Corporation; and Jamestown Laminating Company.

Bruce Erickson and his Fancher Chair Company represent one of the Jamestown area's oldest manufacturing traditions: the furniture industry. The company, named for an English family, has been owned by the Ericksons since the 1970s and makes high quality hand-crafted furniture.

Precision and market awareness

MRC Bearings combines Jamestown's long tradition of precision manufacturing with the international experience and market awareness of Sweden's SKF Group. Jamestown actually began making ball bearing machinery as early as 1902, while SKF was not founded until 1907. In 1986 the Gothenburg-based company, by then a giant worldwide corporation, established a presence in Jamestown when it bought the Bearings Division of TRW and renamed it MRC Bearings. MRC Bearings, the world's largest producer of aerospace bearings, has more than 900 employees today.

Inspecting the outer ring — or "top hat" — of a bearing designed for use in General Electric's GE90, one of three engines selected to power the new twin-engine Boeing 777 widebody aircraft. The complex configuration is accomplished by starting with a 235 pound forging and processing it to a completed ring weight of about 20 pounds.

One of a small number of recent Swedish immigrants who work today at MRC Bearings is Christer Hellstrand from Gothenburg, who is Director of Aerospace Operations.

The beginning of a love affair

Suddenly she is just there, right in front of you... The world's most famous statue. The symbol of freedom, of liberty. Everyone who has seen her recalls that first glimpse. It may have been from the deck of a ship sailing into New York Harbor through the Verrazano Narrows. Or through the window of a car driving in from New Jersey. Or from an airplane window approaching La Guardia, Kennedy or Newark airport. No one forgets that first encounter.

What gives her this magic?
Her torch and upstretched arm?
Her crown?
Her gaze?
Her height?
Not counting her pedestal, at 151 feet she is the tallest modern statue on earth. But her message is even bigger.

One person who is quite familiar with her and the message she embodies appears on the next page. When asked what is perhaps the best single sight that his company can offer, he replies: "It's when we pass the Statue of Liberty in the evening, lower the lights on our boats, and play 'God Bless America.' Then everyone is moved to tears."

"America's Favorite Boat Ride" passing the Brooklyn Bridge.

The circle of life

Among the very first things that Karl Andrén did in 1962 when he arrived as a 15-year-old immigrant in New York — where his father worked at a Swedish shipping company — was to take a Circle Line boat tour. From that day, the magic of this sightseeing line became mixed in with the magic of his youth and his first discovery of Manhattan. But it would take many years before Mr. Andrén closed the circle by becoming the owner of this line, which today has its headquarters along the Hudson River at the foot of West 42nd Street.

Karl Andrén attended Fort Lee High School and Upsala College, Orange, New Jersey. He earned a Master's degree at Penn State (in mineral economics!), started his American working career as a securities analyst on Wall Street, went into corporate finance, raised some money and bought a small tug and barge company in the Port of New York.

This brought him back to his true element. After all, Mr. Andrén's family is from Åland, an archipelago in the Baltic Sea that is inhabited by ethnic Swedes but belongs to Finland. Given its geography and the entrepreneurial spirit of its people, Åland has strong shipping traditions.

Karl's father went to sea when he was thirteen years old and sailed on the old windjammers. Even before the family emigrated to America, Karl himself spent two summers as a deck hand on the Swedish-based Wallenius Line's car carriers, sailing between Europe and the United States.

So Karl Andrén found it natural to own a maritime company, and his new business expanded. But he was not satisfied, because what he really wanted was to buy Circle Line. He talked it over with the company's co-founder and co-owner, Frank Barry. Just after World War II, Mr. Barry had bought up some recently retired landing craft and Coast Guard cutters, painted them red, white and green and started running sightseeing tours from the Battery at the southern tip of Manhattan. Karl Andrén and Frank Barry often saw each other at the Whitehall Lunch Club, a gathering place for shipping executives near the Battery. After many offers and rejections, Mr. Andrén was finally able to take over Circle Line in 1981.

What was then a simple tourist business, based on guided boat trips around Manhattan, has undergone numerous refinements under

Karl Andrén commands his fleet from an office on the bridge of the Circle Line pier, where he combines a sensitivity for the shipping traditions of the Hudson River and New York Harbor with a flair for running a modern floating entertainment, sightseeing and restaurant group.

Karl Andrén. Circle Line is now a part of his New York Cruise Lines, Inc., which also includes World Yacht, Seaport Liberty Cruises (following largely the same route as Circle Line but with departures from South Street Seaport) and Hudson River Dayline (with excursions up the Hudson).

Circle Line's current program includes Harbor Lights sunset cruises, Captain's Club cruises for seniors, "Highlights in Jazz" cruises and other specially tailored excursions. Its sister company World Yacht — the largest luxury restaurant, sightseeing and entertainment concern in New York City — pioneered the concept of "elegant dining afloat." Musicians begin to play as soon as the ship casts off and continue as the cruise slips down the Hudson, around the tip of Manhattan and up the East River to the world-famous Brooklyn Bridge. Just under the bridge, the ship turns around and sails toward the highlight of the trip — the Statue of Liberty. Passing beneath Lady Liberty, the orchestra plays "God Bless America."

All thanks to Karl Andrén, a sailor's son from faraway Åland.

Entrepreneur, inventor and world-class philanthropist Alfred Nobel (1833-1896). Portrait by Emil Österman, courtesy of the Nobel Foundation.

From Nobel to IKEA

Although the Swedish business presence in North America dates primarily from the decades after World War II, its history goes back well over a century. Swedish companies that do business in the United States and Canada have often displayed a sense of ingenuity and adventure that is reminiscent of the Vikings or of 17th century imperial Sweden's desire to establish a bridgehead across the Atlantic. Another element of the mix is the individual emigrant dream of finding a better country, a better market, than one's homeland can offer.

This book examines a cross-section of Swedish innovators, industrialists and business people — the movers and shakers of the entrepreneurial world. We look at individuals who have created Swedish companies in North America, becoming part of the fabric of North American business and society. Many entrepreneurs have arrived in America as representatives of their respective companies. In some cases they have returned home after completing their assigned task. In other cases they have stayed on, becoming naturalized citizens of the United States or Canada.

Dynamic pioneer

The industrialist who built Sweden's first factories outside the domestic market had good reasons for doing so. His name was Alfred Nobel. His products — dynamite and its forerunner, blasting oil (nitroglycerine) — could not be shipped as casually as most other products. The first modern manufacturing plant built abroad by a Swedish-owned company was thus Nobel's blasting oil factory in Krümmel, near Hamburg, Germany, established in 1865. The following year he built a production unit in Norway and one in Little Ferry, New Jersey. The latter was the first Swedish-owned factory in North America.

Alfred Nobel, born in Stockholm in 1833, spent part of his childhood in St. Petersburg, Russia. He was only 17 years old when his father sent him to New York City in 1850. Immanuel Nobel, an industrialist whose company built underwater mines for the Russian navy, wanted his son Alfred to serve an apprenticeship with John Ericsson, a close friend. This was 11 years before Ericsson designed and built the Monitor ironclad vessel during the American Civil War. Alfred Nobel stayed with Ericsson for two years, then went home to St. Petersburg.

Another 14 years passed before Nobel returned to New York, arriving on April 15, 1866. The Civil War was over, and America was bubbling with entrepreneurial spirit. He landed in New York before his epoch-making discovery that mixing a certain kind of sand called kieselguhr with the dangerous nitroglycerine produced a much safer explosive, called dynamite. He made this discovery in Germany, upon his return from America that same autumn. But he arrived in New York around the same time that several major accidents involving blasting oil killed a number of people. As a manufacturer of blasting oil, Alfred Nobel faced the hostility of the American authorities and public opinion. To calm people's fears of nitroglycerine, he personally conducted a well-publicized demonstration of the explosive at a quarry near 83rd Street between Eighth and Ninth Avenues in a then-rural area of upper Manhattan. The demonstration was a major success and attracted a lot of attention, but to many Americans the name Nobel seemed forever destined to be associated with death and horror. It would be interesting to know how deep an impression these confrontations with American public opinion made on Nobel, who willed a huge fortune to support the Nobel Prizes in the sciences, literature and peace.

The main reason why Alfred Nobel was visiting New York was to resolve a patent dispute with a Mr. Shaffner, an unscrupulous Virginia attorney who had claimed the right to Alfred Nobel's American patent on blasting oil. Nobel won the dispute and the two sides declared a temporary truce, joined to form the United States Blasting Oil Company and built the Little Ferry, New Jersey factory in 1866 (it was destroyed by an explosion in 1870). Nobel later transferred his patent rights to the newly created Giant Powder Company, headquartered in San Francisco. In 1868, America's first dynamite factory was built in a canyon just outside of San Francisco (in what is now a city park).

By the time these factories were built, Alfred Nobel had long since left America, to which he never returned. He was disappointed with America: "Life in America was not pleasant to me in the long run. The exaggerated stress over money destroys too many of the pleasures of society and ruins the sense of honor for the sake of imaginary needs," he wrote to a colleague. In time, he phased out all his holdings in America, but he did save a few of his U.S. Blasting Oil stock certificates. "If you need to put new lining in an old overcoat, let me offer you my shares in 'Blasting Oil.' Their color is beautiful," he wrote to a friend.

Here in Little Ferry, on New Jersey's Hackensack River, Alfred Nobel built the first Swedish-owned factory in North America in 1866.

A factory on the Hudson River

Another Swedish company whose first emissaries found the industrialists on the other side of the Atlantic far tougher and more ruthless than they had expected was AB Separator, today a part of Alfa Laval. The company, based on the cream separator invented by the brilliant Gustaf de Laval, was established in Sweden during 1883. That same year, it established its first foreign subsidiary — in America — under the name De Laval Cream Separator Co. It had a number of American shareholders and its offices were located in New York City.

Despite threatened patent disputes, bill-collecting problems and difficulties in finding suitable managers, in 1884 De Laval Cream Separator granted permission for two workshops — one operated by the firm of P.M. Sharples in West Chester, Pennsylvania and the other located in Middletown, Connecticut — to begin production of separators on a subcontracting basis, along Swedish lines.

But De Laval Cream Separator ran into financial difficulties and had to be liquidated. In its place, the De Laval Separator Co. was established, with the Sharples company and other shareholders gaining seats on the board. For a while, AB Separator was close to losing control of its U.S. company, but a new reorganization was implemented. After temporarily manufacturing its separators in Bloomfield, New Jersey, in the autumn of 1892 the company moved its American production activities to a new workshop on the Hudson River in Poughkeepsie, New York.

Sharples and Separator thus split up and had no contact until nearly a century later, in 1988, when Alfa Laval bought Sharples and moved Separation Inc.'s headquarters and much of its centrifuge production operations to the Sharples plant in Warminster, Pennsylvania.

Perhaps the most important reason why Separator and later Alfa Laval were so successful internationally, especially in the U.S. market, was that Gustaf de Laval's designs for the separator were innovative and were continuously being improved by the Swedish company. Although American patents existed in the same field, Separator could honor these patents in the knowledge that its own product was better and that it could preserve its world leadership through product development.

The De Laval Separator Co. workshops along the Hudson River in Poughkeepsie, New York, as they looked in the spring of 1932...

...and a view of the same area today, long after their demolition. In the 1960s, the company's operations moved from this riverfront location to a new site east of Poughkeepsie.

Today Alfa Laval's old "Separator" business in the U.S. is divided into a number of companies. One of these, Alfa Laval Separation Inc., has its base at 955 Mearns Road, Warminster, PA.

Claes Arnegren has directed the transformation of Alfa Laval Separation since the acquisition of Sharples and his company's move to Warminster.

The wingbeats of history

After 1988, when Alfa Laval bought Sharples — the company that became the Swedish group's first American agent in the 1880s — it moved the headquarters for its U.S. separator business to Warminster, Pennsylvania, where Sharples had its main factory. Separator operations, based for decades in Poughkeepsie, New York, have been transformed into a number of more or less independent companies, making them more dynamic as a whole. As early as 1981, Alfa Laval Agri Inc. (milk production and animal breeding equipment) moved to Kansas City. Today the U.S. base of Alfa Laval Flow (pumps, valves, pipe fittings etc. for production systems) — including Alfa Laval Pumps, G&H Products and Tri-Clover Inc. — is located in Kenosha, Wisconsin. In addition, Tri-Clover has a sales and production facility in Brantford, Ontario, Canada. And Alfa Laval Thermal (heat exchangers) has its headquarters and factory in Richmond, Virginia as well as a factory in Newburyport, Massachusetts. Another unit in the Alfa Laval Group is Celleco Inc., which supplies equipment to the process industry and operates a pilot plant for the cleaning of recycled paper at Lawrenceville, Georgia outside Atlanta. For the past several years, Alfa Laval has been part of the Tetra Laval Group, which also includes Tetra Pak. Alfa Laval has about 1,800 employees in North America, including 80 in Canada.

Centrifuge technology remains the core of Alfa Laval Separation's operations today. The company produces the world's largest decanter centrifuges at Warminster, for example.

Slow start for Ericsson

Another Swedish engineering company established during the same era as Separator/Alfa Laval is the Ericsson telecommunications group. Gustaf de Laval actually began manufacturing his first cream separators in 1878, the same year that Lars Magnus Ericsson built his first telephone in Stockholm. But because the telephone was originally invented by an American, Alexander Graham Bell — and the Bell companies strongly dominated the U.S. domestic market — it was not until the deregulation of this market and the advent of cellular telephones that Ericsson got a fair chance to develop a major presence in America (see pages 89-93).

The year that Bell invented his telephone, another Swedish global industrial pioneer entered the U.S. market: Sandvikens Jernverks Aktiebolag (the Sandviken Ironworks Company), established 14 years earlier by Göran Fredrik Göransson. Manning the company's booth at the 1876 U.S. Centennial Exhibition in Philadelphia was his son Albert Göransson, who displayed four railroad wheels complete with axles, a locomotive crankshaft, a steamship crankshaft, a propeller shaft, a steam-driven piston for a forging hammer and samples of various stages of the Bessemer steel-making process (see also pages 68-71).

The company, today called Sandvik, recruited an agent for the U.S. market in 1877. At the 1893 Columbian Exhibition in Chicago, it displayed the longest cold-rolled steel band ever produced at the time. During the early

At the 1893 Columbian Exposition in Chicago, Sandvik displayed the longest cold-rolled steel band of its dimensions ever rolled until that time.

20th century, Sandvik was represented by various U.S. agents, and in December 1919 it established its own sales subsidiary in New York. In 1927 Sandvik also opened an office in Chicago. The year before, it had started the separate Sandvik Watch Spring Company in New York, as well as Sandvik Canadian, Ltd. in Montreal.

Sandvik's aggressive U.S. sales organization and far-flung network of agents (and later offices of its own) served as a model for the overseas ventures of other Swedish industrial enterprises.

Sandsteel Spring Co., Inc. at 145 Hudson Street, New York, 1950.

Before America entered World War I

One company that studied the international sales strategies of both Sandvik and Separator was the bearings specialist Svenska Kullagerfabriken, established in 1907 in Gothenburg. SKF began building up its own international organization, focusing initially on the British and U.S. markets. Sven Wingquist, the company's founder, traveled to the United States in the autumn of 1909 and personally established a sales subsidiary, SKF Ball Bearing Company, in New York. Two years later he returned to plan a U.S. ball bearing factory, but concluded that the time was not yet ripe. He nevertheless made sure to establish another sales office, in Chicago. In November 1914 Wingquist sent a representative to New York to reorganize SKF's American operations and arrange to have a factory built. Hartford, Connecticut was chosen as the site, and construction of the factory began in the autumn of 1915. The following year, another business opportunity arose. SKF bought a majority holding in the American ball bearing maker Hess-Bright Manufacturing, which also sold Deutsche Waffenfabrik's bearings in America and had a brand-new factory in Philadelphia. (It later also acquired the German company's shares in Hess-Bright.) In April 1917 the U.S. broke with Germany, declared war against the Axis powers and began a full mobilization. By then, both factories had plenty of orders. The young SKF had gained a stable platform in North America. Today SKF has 22 U.S. factories. It has about 6,900 employees in North America (see page 46).

The interwar period

During the two decades between World War I and World War II, Swedish international corporations consolidated their position. Only two important new entrepreneurs emerged on the world stage during the 1920s. One was the industrialist and financier Ivar Kreuger, who built up Swedish Match into a worldwide corporate empire before being ruined by the financial crash and committing suicide in 1932. The other was Axel Wenner-Gren, whose sales of vacuum cleaners and later refrigerators laid the groundwork for Electrolux, which in 1956 became part of the Wallenberg Group.

The SKF plant in Gainesville, Georgia has put a lot of effort into improving the environment, both indoors and outdoors.

SKF's first factory in North America was built in Hartford, Connecticut in 1915-1916.

SKF's newest U.S. factory will produce hub units in Aiken, South Carolina, as part of efforts to bolster the company's position as a supplier to the American automotive industry.

SKF's new investments in North America also include a technical development center in Detroit, Michigan.

The new wave

The next major wave of Swedish companies entered the North American market only in the 1960s. If any pioneering postwar ventures in North America can be compared with the unique business undertakings of the late 19th century, it is the Swedish product launches that began cautiously in the mid-1950s. This was when the first Volvo cars were sold in the United States through local dealerships in California and Texas, and later by Volvo's own representatives on the east coast.

Volvo's top executive at that time, Gunnar Engellau, had a very optimistic view of the American market. After the first few years of successful test sales, the Volvo board simply decided that its aim was to make North America the company's second domestic market. In June 1963 Volvo was the first European car maker to establish its own assembly plant in North America — first in Dartmouth, Nova Scotia, Canada, and then across the harbor in Halifax. Ten years later, Volvo announced plans to build an automotive plant in the United States as well, having acquired the necessary land in Chesapeake, Virginia. A plant was built, but no cars were produced there. The 1973-74 oil crisis had suddenly turned the market situation of the world's auto companies upside down. Instead, part of the Chesapeake facility has been used for the production of Volvo Penta marine engines.

Volvo's success in the North American car market inspired major investments in trucks as well. Sten Langenius, then President of Volvo Truck Corporation, spent a year in Greensboro, North Carolina working with Thage Berggren, head of the company's U.S. truck operations at the time, to launch Volvo's new venture in the U.S. heavy vehicle market. Early in 1988 Volvo took over the heavy truck range of General Motors. A new company — Volvo GM Heavy Trucks — was established, with Volvo holding 76 percent and GM 24 percent (now 87-13). See pages 94-95.

General Motors is also a 50-50 partner with Investor AB in another well-known Swedish vehicle maker, Saab Automobile. In a recent reorganization, this Swedish-based company moved its U.S. headquarters from Connecticut to the Atlanta area. With many of its new executives having been recruited from GM's

Volvo's American heroes #2 and #3: Thage Berggren (left) and Sten Langenius, who built up Volvo Truck Corporation's sales and operations in the United States during the early 1980s.

Volvo's American Hero #1: During most of the 1970s and 1980s, Björn Ahlström headed Volvo North America, which at the time included cars, marine engines and heavy trucks. He was the man who implemented the Volvo board's decisions to make North America the automotive group's second domestic market for cars. Meanwhile his example inspired many other Swedish corporate executives in North America to launch their own aggressive ventures. He has remained faithful to his new homeland; an American citizen, he lives in New Jersey.

The headquarters of Volvo Cars of North America's in Rockleigh, New Jersey.

Much of the engineering know-how that Volvo accumulates in the course of its car production work is made available to other companies via the subsidiary Olofström Automation Ltd. (established through the amalgamation of the Olofström Automation Division of Volvo Canada Ltd. and the Canadian Export Tool & Welding Co.). This company has its headquarters in Mississauga outside Toronto, Canada (below) as well as a presence in Detroit.

Among Volvo's large recent investments in North America was the acquisition of Canadian bus manufacturer Prévost Car Inc. — a joint venture with the British-based Henlys Group — during the summer of 1995.

Family patriarch Peter Wallenberg (right), is the 1996 recipient of the America's Swede Of the Year Award. Here he is presenting Sweden's King Carl XVI Gustaf with a 50th birthday gift.

Saturn division, Saab is now launching a renewed sales drive in North America and other markets.

The Wallenberg family, which has dominated Swedish industry and finance since the second half of the 19th century, has drawn a great deal of inspiration from America over the decades. The founder of Stockholms Enskilda Bank, which became part of Skandinaviska Enskilda Banken, was André Oscar Wallenberg (1816-1886), son of the Church of Sweden's bishop of Linköping, Marcus Wallenberg. As a newly commissioned naval officer in 1835, A.O. Wallenberg found it hard to break into the privileged circles in the royal capital of Stockholm. He took a job in the merchant marine, with Boston as his base, sailing both on trans-Atlantic and smaller coastal and river vessels. At times he supported himself, under an assumed name, as a stevedore in American ports.

The experiences and impressions that A.O. Wallenberg brought home after his years in America, which lasted until the mid-1840s (before mass emigration from Sweden began) were naturally very important to his own future actions and those of his family in the Swedish business world.

Today the Wallenberg industrial holding company, Investor AB, owns Saab, 50 percent of Saab Automobile and a portfolio of major holdings in a number of Sweden's largest, most internationally active industrial groups. These include major shareholdings in such companies as Scania, Astra, Incentive (and through it ABB), Stora, Ericsson, Atlas Copco, SKF, and Electrolux. From their central posts in the bank, Investor and the boards of the various companies, Wallenberg family members have played a key role in the expansion of Sweden's commercial ties with other countries, not least North America.

Numerous acquisitions

More as a rule than an exception, both Wallenberg Group companies and other Swedish-based enterprises have chosen to enter the North American market with the help of a partner or by acquiring a local company. Especially during the 1970s and 1980s, the Swedes were involved in numerous U.S. acquisitions or joint ventures.

In 1976, for example, the Swedish-based office products group Esselte bought America's Oxford Pendaflex and in 1978 Dymo Industries. During the 1970s, the Perstorp chemical group began a major international expansion which included a number of acquisitions in North America and the construction of a new laminate flooring factory in North Carolina (see page 122).

Not to mention Electrolux with a string of North American acquisitions, among them National Union Electric (vacuum cleaners) in 1974, Tappan (ovens etc.) in 1979, White (household appliances) and Poulan/Weed Eater (forest and garden equipment) in 1986, American Yard Products in 1988 and Allegretti & Co. in 1990 (garden equipment). See pages 100-103.

Other strategic acquisitions in recent decades included AGA's purchase of Burdox in 1978. This represented a return to the American market, which AGA had originally entered as early as 1911 by establishing American Gas Accumulator in New Jersey (see pages 74-75).

In 1981 Tarkett took a giant step across the Atlantic by purchasing the North American and European flooring operations of GAF (see pages 60-61). Tetra Pak's 1986 acquisition of the Minnesota-based Liquipak greatly accelerated the North American expansion it had already begun (see pages 78-80). And during the 1990s, ASSA Abloy's purchase of U.S.-based Arrow

Lock and later Essex Holdings made it the world's leading lock company (see page 63).

Other major Swedish corporations that have greatly enlarged their North American presence by means of acquisitions are the heavy equipment manufacturer Atlas Copco (pages 86-88), the construction company Skanska (pages 106-109), the medical technology specialist Gambro (pages 120-121) and to a lesser extent Ericsson (pages 89-93).

In 1985, Volvo's construction equipment unit joined forces with America's Clark Equipment Company to establish Volvo Michigan Euclid (VME). In 1995, however, Volvo bought out Clark and changed the company's name to Volvo Construction Equipment (pages 96-97).

One high-profile enterprise that started off in North America on a franchising basis but also eventually decided that it could conquer the continent on its own power is the IKEA home furnishings chain. Like some of the other Swedish corporations presented in this book, IKEA established operations in Canada before venturing cautiously into the U.S. market. Today the company seems almost big enough to furnish all the empty bedrooms, kitchens and living rooms in the country (pages 132-133).

Have a nice trip!

So let us continue our trip across the North American continent. Along the way, we will encounter many of the above-mentioned companies, and others as well. We will meet a wide variety of entrepreneurs, products and milieus. Starting on the east coast, we will swing through Boston and south toward New Jersey and Washington, D.C., then veer off toward the Midwest, especially the Chicago area. After that, aside from a few quick forays into Canada, we move down to the southern states, north again through Colorado, over the Rockies and into California, ending our journey in Seattle. You will notice how the companies change character, depending both on geographic location and industry.

After touring the west coast — with its emphasis on individualism — we present a gallery of leading Swedish-American personalities and round off the book with a glimpse of the future.

It is time to let you begin this transcontinental journey on your own power. Feel free to do so at whatever speed you find comfortable and by whatever alternative or roundabout route you prefer. Have a nice trip!

It's a big country. Someone's got to furnish it. IKEA

Feet planted firmly on the floor

Ingvar Backhamre has seldom doubted where he stands, physically or mentally. In other words, his feet are planted firmly on the floor. After all, floors are his business. There was a time, though, when Mr. Backhamre was not really sure where he lived. That was back in 1981, when he was commuting back and forth frequently across the Atlantic as Tarkett's representative while negotiating to buy the unprofitable North American and European flooring operations of GAF.

"For almost a whole year, I was living with my inner clock on 'mid-Atlantic time,'" he explained. Once the acquisition was completed, Ingvar Backhamre settled down in a new home. He became an American in every sense, establishing a new U.S. business headquarters for Tarkett and himself in Parsippany, New Jersey less than an hour by car from Manhattan. From there, he oversees sales and production at the company's factories in Whitehall, Pennsylvania and Vails Gate, New York.

As president and CEO of Tarkett Inc., Mr. Backhamre has streamlined manufacturing, negotiated with unions, implemented two difficult turn-arounds and carved out new market segments in resilient flooring — from high-end sheet vinyl products to mid-priced products. He has established strategic alliances, for example with Mohawk, the second largest carpet company in North America.

In the course of more than 30 years at Tarkett, Ingvar Backhamre has served under four presidents and five different owners. During his years in America, some of Tarkett's competitors have switched presidents 4-6 times. He is an entrepreneur who defends his independence and that of his company within the framework of a large corporation.

What keeps him in such good trim? "You must deliver the results and the profits, otherwise the owner doesn't want you to stay. You must be a very positive person, or the problems will wear you down. You must change all the time and understand that what was right in the past may not be right any more,." Ingvar Backhamre replies.

Making locks requires concentration and precision. The skilled production workers at the New Haven factory can draw on many generations of metalworking expertise.

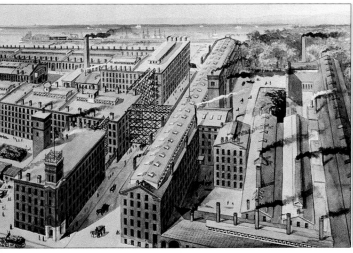

As the man responsible for Assa Abloy's operations in the United States, Clas Thelin has led the task of merging the Swedish-based group with Essex. Today his headquarters are at the modern Sargent Essex facility in New Haven, where various pictures on the wall remind the visitor that the New Haven company's traditions stretch back to New England's industrial revolution.

Unlocking a key market

In metalworking, the transition from craft to industry began in Europe and quickly spread to North America, with New England as an early bridgehead. Cities like Hartford and New Haven, Connecticut were among the first centers of the U.S. metalworking industry.

In 1810, for example, one Joseph D. Sargent started a hardware business that eventually led to a metal products company — Sargent Manufacturing, today in its second century in New Haven and the city's largest single industrial enterprise. After a series of mergers, Sargent became part of Essex Holdings, which also includes Curries Company and Graham Manufacturing, two Mason City, Iowa-based makers of steel and wood doors; and McKinney Products, a Scranton, Pennsylvia-based maker of hinges.

Let us now move to Scandinavia and back in time to the year 1732. Finland was still part of Sweden. The Stockholm-born Michael Hising established a helve hammer and forge in Björkboda, Finland, where the manufacture of locks began some 150 years later (in 1887). Lock production had meanwhile started around 1848 in Sweden's most important metalwork-

ing center, Eskilstuna. The corporate descendents of these small Björkboda and Eskilstuna enterprises eventually merged in 1994 to create Assa Abloy, one of the world's leading lock manufacturers.

For years, companies in what is now Assa Abloy were active in certain niches of the U.S. market: Assa with its high security cylinders, Abloy with its industrial and cam locks and VingCard with recodable hotel locks. The acquisition of New York-based Arrow Lock was a first step toward a more complete market presence, then late in 1995, Assa Abloy made headlines with another trans-Atlantic merger: its purchase of the privately held Essex Holdings.

This is how a number of modest craft-based enterprises in various parts of Europe and America have now come together to form the world's leading lock company, with around 6,000 employees. Cross-fertilization between the European and American technologies and product ranges in the new group has only just begun. And for Assa Abloy, the purchase of a large, well-established U.S. company in its field will help unlock the biggest market of them all.

Following the immigrants

In the early 1870s a growing number of Swedish immigrants began settling around Worcester, Massachusetts. The first groups of Swedes to settle in New England had arrived in Brockton in 1851. When Norton Company (a leading manufacturer of grinding machinery and abrasives) was founded in Worcester in 1885, the influx of Swedes accelerated. By the outbreak of World War I, about 75 percent of the workers at this large company were of Swedish extraction.

Of course no one was thinking about any of this in the 1940s when Astra, the Swedish pharmaceuticals company, began the task of gaining the approval of the American authorities to market its revolutionary local anesthetic, Xylocaine®. Astra Pharmaceutical Products Inc. established its office at 11 East 77th Street in New York City. Late in 1948, the Food and Drug Administration gave the green light for Xylocaine. The company decided to launch the drug primarily as an anesthetic for use in dentists' offices.

The man responsible for this U.S. market launch, Börje Jalar, had a brother who was a dentist in Worcester, MA, so he moved the Astra office there. The task of marketing Xylocaine in Canada also began from Worcester, but Astra's Canadian operations later became independent. Early in 1955, the first Canadian-made Xylocaine cartridges were delivered from Astra Canada's own production facility in Toronto. Today Astra Canada is one of that country's five largest pharmaceutical enterprises, having opened a new factory in Toronto and a research lab in Montreal.

Astra USA Inc. has long since "outgrown" its original Worcester office. Its futuristic, continuously expanding corporate headquarters and plants are located in Westborough, MA, between Worcester and Boston. Here, too, many Swedish-Americans are among the employees.

Whereas Astra Canada today sells products from the Astra Group's entire range, two separate marketing channels were built up in the United States. Prilosec®, an ulcer medicine based in part on the Xylocaine-related research work, the blood pressure medicine Plendil® and other drugs are marketed via the half-owned Astra Merck Inc. Meanwhile Astra USA Inc. itself has focused on the hospital market, selling Astra's anesthetic and analgesic products as well as such critical care pharmaceuticals as Streptase®, which is used to dissolve blood clots; Foscavir®, used for the treatment of

CMV retinitis; and injectable multivitamins. In recent years, Astra USA Inc. has also developed new pharmaceuticals for the outpatient care market, including Toprol-XL® for the treatment of hypertension and various other cardiovascular conditions, as well as such anti-asthma agent delivery systems as the Pulmicort Turbuhaler®.

Using the Astra Group's corporate symbol — a stylized, pyramid-like A — on a vast scale, Astra USA Inc. moved into this new corporate headquarters building in Westborough, Massachusetts, after outgrowing its offices in nearby Worcester. Many Swedish-Americans work here.

Going with the cash flow

Ever since the day in 1981 when Skandinaviska Enskilda Banken opened its own office in New York, it has been located on Park Avenue. This also seems to be the way in which S-E-Banken has always staked out its territory: by placing itself in the heart of a city. In its home country, Sweden, S-E-Banken has for many decades been the leading commercial bank for major export-oriented corporations. It has also been the house bank of the Wallenberg family, with its far-flung industrial and commercial interests. In historical terms, S-E-Banken is a descendant of a bank originally founded by the Wallenbergs in the mid-19th century.

In New York, S-E-Banken today operates mainly as a Nordic-oriented bank. Its primary target groups are the American subsidiaries of companies based in the Nordic region (Denmark, Finland, Iceland, Norway and Sweden) as well as American companies that do business in that region and financial institutions that invest in Nordic securities and currencies.

A separate S-E-Bank Group company, Enskilda Securities Inc., is responsible for investment banking operations, including equities trading. It also handles mergers and acquisitions through an alliance with the American-based Blackstone.

The head of S-E-Banken's New York office is Johan Stern (photo right above), who oversees a commercial banking operation with an extensive battery of services from lending to cash management. The bank specializes in bringing together the cash flows of clients' American operations with those of their operations elsewhere in the world. The bank's other major field of activity is trading and capital markets, which includes currencies and a variety of financial instruments. The New York office also handles the bank's own funding and clearing of U.S. dollar payments for the entire S-E-Bank Group.

S-E-Banken's Park Avenue trading room is a strong link in the bank's 24-hour global trading in currencies and other financial instruments. The office also handles the S-E-Bank Group's dollar clearing and is one of the top 25 players in New York.

Hard metals, easy touch

In 1876 Sandvik was a 14-year-old provincial steelworks in northern Sweden when the company made its American debut at the U.S. Centennial Exhibition in Philadelphia. Its exhibit focused on the wondrous steel products emerging from Sandvik's furnaces after it became the first company in the world to apply the Bessemer method on an industrial scale. The Sandvik name was on everyone's lips at the exhibition. Sandvik steel reached North America in the form of wires, cold-rolled steel products, spring steel, hardened conveyor belts and finished products like handsaws, clock springs and razor blades. Stainless steel and Sandvik Coromant cemented carbide products arrived later. Sandvik is among the few global corporations that have managed for more than a century to combine a knowledge and feel for specialized products with an openness and sensitivity to customer needs. The group also began at an early stage to build up its own organization in North America for both sales and production.

The headquarters of Sandvik, Inc. in Fair Lawn, New Jersey oversees an organization with companies in Fair Lawn, NJ (Coromant); Asheville, North Carolina (Dormer Tools and Union Butterfield Corp.); Houston, Texas (Sandvik Rock Tools); Warren, Michigan (Sandvik Hard Materials); Scranton, Pennsylvania (Sandvik Steel Co., Pennsylvania Extruded Tube Co., Sandvik Saws and Tools Co.); Kennewick, Washington (Sandvik Special Metals Corp.); Branford, Connecticut (Sandvik Milford Corp.); Milan, Tennessee (Sandvik Windsor Corp.); Totowa, New Jersey (Sandvik Process Systems, Inc.); and Louisville, Kentucky (Sandvik Sorting Systems, Inc.). And as if this were not enough, Sandvik Latin America, Inc. oversees its markets from Coral Gables, Florida. And a Coromant warehouse in Erlanger, Kentucky provides next-day deliveries all over North America. These are a few hard facts about Sandvik, Inc., a company that displays an easy touch in its customer relations.

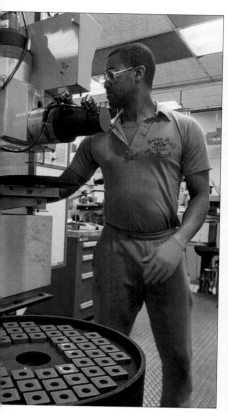

Sandvik is the world market leader in the manufacture of cemented carbide cutting tools, with more than 35,000 standard products plus an extensive line of Tailor Made products.

The U.S. headquarters of Sandvik Coromant Company and of the holding company Sandvik, Inc. are located in Fair Lawn, NJ, with James T. Baker (above) as President and CEO of both.

A seamless tube literally being drawn from a piece of steel at Pennsylvania Extruded Tube Co. (Pexco) in Scranton.

An overnight sensation

Sandvik Sorting Systems and its parent division, Sandvik Process Systems, are unique in the worldwide Sandvik Group. While most other Sandvik companies work with a broad range of metal products, Sandvik Sorting is primarily a designer and integrator of customized sorting systems for overnight package services, airports and similar workplaces. In 1901 Sandvik was the first company to make steel belts, and it has used this knowledge to carve a niche for itself as the technological leader in automated sorting systems.

Sandvik gained a strategic position in the U.S. market for such installations when it acquired Seamco, a Louisville-based manufacturer of package sorting systems that had been established in 1956. Today Sandvik Sorting Systems has nearly 250 employees, about half of whom work at a modern facility near downtown Louisville. Their task includes not only designing and manufacturing systems that meet the needs of each particular location, but also providing full integration of hardware and software as well as conducting tests and training. Sandvik's systems help its customers achieve higher capacities while decreasing costs. Due to this and other benefits, Sandvik Sorting Systems is projecting significant growth in the near future.

One of the largest installations delivered by Sandvik Sorting Systems was this Federal Express facility at Newark Airport, New Jersey (large photo). Both hardware and software, including the control and monitoring systems (inset on the right), were custom-designed and installed by the Louisville-based company.

The engineers at the design department in Louisville work in project teams that customize each individual delivery.

President Hermann Miedel (inset in the middle) runs Sandvik Sorting Systems in a youthful, independent entrepreneurial spirit.

Swedish turboprops take off in America

It was one of the most courageous steps in Swedish industrial history when Saab decided in the late 1970s to invest in the production of civilian commuter aircraft. Founded in the 1930s to supply the Swedish Air Force, Saab eventually found itself having to identify new markets to offset the decline in military orders. With only a tiny domestic market for civilian aircraft, Saab targeted foreign airlines. The United States alone was expected to account for half of the world market for commuter aircraft once the deregulation of the civil aviation was completed. Saab decided to establish a presence there.

Saab, a relatively small aircraft manufacturer from a small country, sent over its most accomplished aircraft sales staff to organize a marketing campaign. Meanwhile it established a partnership with Fairchild Industries, an American manufacturer of commuter aircraft, set up an initial base of operations on Long Island and opened a marketing organization in Paris.

The plan was successful. In 1985, however, the Saab-Fairchild partnership ended and Saab took over the entire program. The first civilian aircraft developed by the partnership is now the world's largest-selling regional turboprop, the Saab 340. Major customers have included American Eagle, the regional affiliate of American Airlines. Saab Aircraft has also developed a larger commuter aircraft with room for 50 passengers, the Saab 2000 — a turboprop with jet-like performance and one of the most modern aircraft in the market — thanks to collaboration with sister company Saab Military Aircraft, manufacturer of one of the world's most technologically advanced military aircraft, the JAS 39 Gripen. Aside from the United States, the Saab 2000 is flown in Europe by airlines in Switzerland, Germany and France, among others. And if you fly between the Marshall Islands in the Pacific, chances are it will be on a Saab 2000.

Saab Aircraft's American subsidiary — which handles marketing, after sales services and parts — is based in Sterling, Virginia, near Dulles International Airport, and has about 75 employees.

N5123L

Saab Aircraft of America Inc.

Patrick F. Murphy (left) and his predecessor as President and CEO of AGA Gas, Inc., Åke Nyborg, are two entrepreneurs who work within the framework of a major corporation.

Keeping it light

In 1904 AGA was founded as a gas company by Sweden's Gustaf Dalén, who was awarded the 1912 Nobel Prize in physics "for his invention of automatic regulators for use in conjunction with gas accumulators for illuminating lighthouses and buoys." Industrial gas remains AGA's core business today. In 1911 the company's first operation outside Sweden was established in New Jersey under the name American Gas Accumulator. The following year, AGA made its first big international breakthrough by landing the contract to build a lighthouse system for the Panama Canal.

After World War II, however, AGA decided to withdraw from the American gas market. American Gas Accumulator was sold. Not until 1978 did the Swedish company, by then a major multinational group in its field, make an American comeback by acquiring Burdox Inc., a local industrial gas company in Cleveland. From this base, AGA has methodically enlarged its U.S. clientele by establishing new service centers and retail stores around the Midwest. The company not only sells industrial gases, but also a complete line of welding and cutting equipment and supplies. To throw a bit more light on the subject, this is part of a carefully conceived long-term strategy which also includes developing and introducing new gas-based technologies in such traditional Midwestern industries as steel, rubber and glass — thereby increasing their productivity and making them more competitive in today's global market. AGA Gas, Inc. also provides services to the chemical, petrochemical, pharmaceutical, food processing, electronics and automotive industries.

AGA Gas Inc.'s largest air separation plant is located in Canton, Ohio.

A sigh of relief

Sten Gibeck drew a sigh of relief in 1988 when the acquisition of the American medical technology company Dryden Corporation in Indianapolis was completed. The purchase gave his company a solid base for expansion in North America. In 1986 Mr. Gibeck and his family had moved temporarily to Chicago to launch the family business's products in the American market. The Swedish Trade Council office in Chicago played a helpful role in this process.

The product that Sten Gibeck was preparing to launch in the world market was an "artificial nose": a heat and moisture exchanger (HME) for medical use during anesthesia and in the respiratory care of laryngectomy and tracheotomy patients. Sten Gibeck began building up his company around this device and a range of other medical equipment. Today the Gibeck Group operates in Europe, North America and the Far East. It has focused on three business segments: 1) anesthesia, respiratory and intensive care, 2) ventilator care in nursing facilities and at home and 3) products for laryngectomy and tracheotomy patients. Gibeck Inc., which is responsible for both the North and South American markets, manufactures airway systems devices and products to prevent contamination in airway systems. The company, located on the prairie outside of Indianapolis, Indiana, is doing nicely and represents close to 50 percent of Gibeck Group sales.

Gibeck, Inc. manufactures products in the field of airways systems. These gas sampling lines are used for CO_2 monitoring during anesthesia.

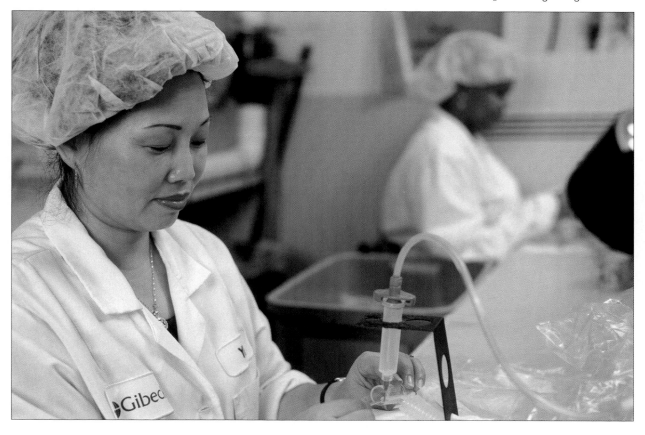

Sten Gibeck, shown here holding a Humid-Vent heat and moisture exchanger (HME), is an entrepreneur from Stockholm who gave his medical equipment company a permanent U.S. address on the prairie outside Indianapolis. With him is Bob Ricks, President of Gibeck, Inc.

Where ideas become reality

Few companies make products that succeed in becoming an integral part of a country's culture. And although people may not immediately associate the name Tetra Pak with the American way of life, the company's packaging systems for individual portions of fruit juice, chocolate or white milk have in fact become part of the daily lives of millions of American school children. A Tetra Brik® Aseptic package of fruit juice and a granola bar are a classic American snack.

Ruben Rausing (1894-1983), the founder of Tetra Pak, had no childhood memories of his own from the United States, but his entire business career was strongly influenced by the years he spent at Columbia University in New York, where he earned a Master of Science degree in 1920. During this period, he was first exposed to "self-service" stores and realized that this concept would eventually be adopted in Europe, thus increasing the demand for pre-packaged goods. Dr. Rausing built several companies that were based on his packaging concepts. Perhaps the best known is Tetra Pak, a family business established in 1951 in Lund, Sweden. The company took its name from the tetrahedron-shaped (or four-sided) cartons it pioneered. In 1963 it launched its Tetra Brik Aseptic carton. The company's first commercial contact with the American market was an agreement with the Milliken Corporation to market the tetrahedron-shaped carton packaging system in the U.S. Milliken Tetra Pak was establsihed and a packaging material factory was built at White Stone, South Carolina.

But it took time before the Tetra Brik Aseptic system made its real breakthrough in Ameri-

The Tetra Pak Research Center is one of the most advanced facilities of its kind in the world in terms of its laboratory, equipment, product information resources and staff of experts. It has a variety of the latest ultra-high temperature (UHT) process equipment such as plate, tubular and scraped surface heat exchangers and a direct steam injection system The glow in the large photo comes from the ultraviolet light used in the disinfection process.

ca. Tetra Pak's first major success with this new packaging concept came in European and Asian markets. By 1974 the company was preparing to enter the North American market via Canada, where the dairy company Laiterie Cité introduced the Tetra Brik Aseptic system. And in 1977 the Tetra Brik Aspetic package was launched in the U.S. market by the newly established Brik Pak, Inc. Not until 1981, however, did the system received the approval of the U.S. Food and Drug Administration. After that, Tetra Pak was able to launch its packaging systems on a large scale in the United States. In 1984 it completed a new plant for the production of packaging material in Denton, Texas. Another factory was built in Canada the following year.

In 1986 Tetra Pak greatly speeded up the process of expanding its U.S. presence by acquiring Liquipak, a company in St. Paul, Minnesota that manufactured gable-top cartons. Today it is Tetra Rex Packaging Systems Inc. In 1989 Tetra Pak MatWest, a factory in Vancouver, Washington, was established for the production of gable-top packaging. And these steps were followed by others.

Today Tetra Pak employs about 1,000 people in the United States and 300 in Canada at a total of eight factories. The group's U.S. headquarters is located in Chicago; the Canadian headquarters in Aurora, Ontario; and the regional head office for both North and South America in Atlanta, Georgia.

One indication of the role of the North American market in Tetra Pak's strategic planning came in 1992 when the group moved its research and development work for Tetra Rex packaging machines from Sweden to the U.S., the most competitive market for gable-top packaging. Among other things, this was the starting point for the Tetra Pak Research Center, located in Buffalo Grove, Illinois, outside Chicago.

The Tetra Pak Research Center is an integrated one-stop product development facility for processing and packaging systems that handle fruit juice, concentrates, milk, soups, wine and soy products as well as viscous products such as salad dressings and puddings. More than just a testing facility, it also provides employees of customer companies with hands-on, full-scale training before new equipment start-ups. These photos show the laboratory in action, among other things monitoring the process in a packaging machine.

Exporting a package solution

Nefab, a small company founded in 1923 in Hälsingland, northern Sweden, today has grown into a multinational organization with a presence in 15 countries. One of its most successful products is a kind of collapsible case made of laminates and steel, which it developed in the late 1960s in cooperation with Ericsson, the giant Swedish-based telecommunications group. All those who came into contact with this packaging system understood that it offered a high-quality, economical solution for industrial and international shippers.

In 1984, Nefab successfully exported its packaging systems across the Atlantic when the company bought a factory in Peterborough, Ontario, Canada (inset), and began to target the North American export industry. Today Chicago-based Nefab, Inc. employs more than 60 people and serves major customers in the telecommunications, automotive, chemical and machinery industries. Its two main products, NEFAB ExPak and NEFAB RePak, cover virtually every need for reliable, cost-efficient packaging for transport and storage. Due to increased demand for Nefab's environmentally friendly packaging, the company is now experiencing rapid growth.

Jan Sjöström, President of Nefab, Inc., came to the United States at age 17 from Lidingö, Sweden. An athletic scholarship enabled him to study international economics while training as an elite swimmer at the University of Southern California (USC) in Los Angeles. He competed in international events as a member of the Swedish national swimming team. Today he is in charge of the team that is coordinating Nefab's successful North American offensive.

Food for thought

There are many paths to success. But those who read this book a bit thoughtfully will notice one recurring pattern: a person who bases his career on his own life experiences and social heritage, and who applies his talents generously for the benefit of others, will often go a long way. Take Jack Berntson, for example. He was born in Chicago, where his father was a carpenter and his mother ran a grocery shop. In 1935 the family moved home to Sweden, where his father became a building contractor and his mother opened her own country store.

What did Jack, who grew up partly in the United States and partly in Sweden, do with his life? One source of stability had always been working among all the goods that his mother sold in her stores. He had helped her out many times, among fragrant shelves of coffee and other groceries. So Jack Berntson eventually became the man who introduced Swedish specialty foods to large portions of North America. Moving back to the U.S. in 1955, he spent many years driving thousands of miles from state to state — selling lingonberries, Swedish coffee, ginger snaps, specialty canned meats and fish, and crispbreads.

His company, Skandia Foods, Inc., grew into the largest seller of Scandinavian foods in the U.S. and a leading Midwestern importer-distributor of perishable and dry specialty foods. In 1987 he sold the company to a holding company owned by Société Roquefort and Group Perrier, both of France. In the early 1990s the French company sold Skandia Foods and its other U.S. food distributors to Distribution Plus Inc. (DPI), owned by the Irish Dairy Board. Being part of a larger group gives him greater resources and a bigger market, enabling more people to benefit from his talents. Jack Berntson now has even more goods to work with. His warehouse in Arlington Heights outside Chicago is full of fragrant coffees and other groceries, and he is still the boss. Not a bad story, if you think about it.

This Nicolet, Quebec direct current filter yard — whose reactors and capacitator banks prevent small harmonic currents from flowing into the DC line — is only one of many technologically advanced features of the Quebec-New England Multiterminal HVDC Project.

A transformation process

Business, like technology, is a never-ending process of transformation. Those who want to survive must find strategies that prove sustainable in the future. In the midst of our daily activities, we have little sense of where we are in this process. Let us look at the history of one of the world's largest, most powerful corporations — ABB, which was created by the 1988 merger between Sweden's ASEA and Switzerland's Brown Boveri. Both companies were born during the wave of technological development in which Thomas A. Edison's light bulb, Charles F. Brush's electric dynamo and George Westing-

house's alternating current equipment were important milestones. ASEA was established in 1883, with a Swedish dynamo as its first product. Brown Boveri's oldest roots go back to Oerlikon, a company founded in 1882 (Brown Boveri itself was established in 1891). Americans strongly dominated the electric power business, and European companies in this field stayed away from the North American market for many years.

At a relatively early stage, however, before World War I, ASEA had begun to sell generators in Canada. After the Armistice, it tried to break into the U.S. market by selling motors via a small American electrical engineering company, Crocker-Wheeler. General Electric, the U.S.-based giant that had emerged from Edison's companies and other enterprises, was displeased and the prospective motor sales company turned down the Swedish agency assignment. During the 1920s General Electric initiated a general offensive against its European competitors. This included a 1929 attempt to buy its way into ASEA, which was repulsed. The shares that GE had bought were later sold to Sweden's Wallenberg Group.

ASEA did, however, have one electrical engineering specialty in which domestic American competition was not so heavy — relays. It built up a U.S. sales organization during the interwar period. After World War II, ASEA became even more courageous and began selling condensers and surge diverters in the U.S. via a company called Ohio Brass. Other ASEA specialties that found their way into the North American market were mine hoists and electric furnaces.

During the 1960s ASEA began to establish a leading world position in high voltage direct current (HVDC) transmission. In a multi-stage joint venture with General Electric during the late 1960s and part of the 1970s, ASEA built what was then the world's largest power transmission system of its kind, the Pacific Intertie, from the Columbia River hundreds of miles south to Los Angeles. Later came a similar project on the east coast, when the first large-scale multiterminal HVDC system in the world, the Hydro Québec-New England Hydro project, was finalized. It involved the transmission of direct current from Radisson, Quebec — located at the southern end of Hudson Bay — to Sandy Pond, Massachusetts, outside Boston. By

then, however, the supplier was not called ASEA but ABB Power Systems.

Well before beginning deliveries to the latter project, in 1970 ASEA had established a factory at Varennes, outside Montreal, Quebec, to manufacture large transformers. In the same year, ASEA and America's RTE formed a joint venture for the manufacture of mid-sized transformers in Waukesha near Milwaukee, Wisconsin — a factory that ABB later had to divest for competitive reasons as part of its acquisition of Westinghouse's power transmission operations.

ASEA's strategy in the early 1980s also included local manufacturing in several other product areas. In 1982, for example, in partnership with America's Harnischfeger Corporation, ASEA started a whole new factory for industrial automation, motor operating systems and electronic equipment for the process indus-

Industrial landmarks built by ASEA: The transformer factory in Varennes, Quebec dating from 1970 (below) and one of two New Berlin, Wisconsin factories established in 1982 (below right).

These glimpses from ABB factories in New Berlin show two types of equipment builders, each with their own advantages: humans and industrial robots.

try in New Berlin outside Milwaukee. On an adjacent lot, it meanwhile built a new industrial robot factory. Today these factories are part of ABB Inc.'s Industrial and Building Systems segment. Like ABB's other U.S. segments — Power Generation, Power Transmission and Distribution, and Financial Services — the Industrial and Building Systems segment reports to ABB's U.S. headquarters in Norwalk, Connecticut. Other ABB operations in the U.S. include ABB Lummus Global, ABB Vetco Gray and the joint ABB Daimler-Benz transportation venture ADtranz. In the United States alone, ABB employs some 22,000 people in approximately 50 factories and more than 300 sales and service centers. ABB's Canadian operations have more than 2,000 employees at 10 production facilities and at some two dozen other locations. But don't rely on this mid-1996 snapshot for too long. Like the electrical currents pulsing through its products, ABB is in a never-ending process of transformation.

Sune Ericson, Vice President, General Industry, is one of the Swedish-born veterans at ABB in New Berlin, Wisconsin.

Keeping up the pressure

Atlas Copco, one of Sweden's oldest engineering companies (founded in 1873), waited a long time before establishing a presence on the North American continent, which was dominated by large domestic competitors. Once it did so, the starting point was Canada. Before World War II, Atlas Copco operated an engine sales company there. The group also established its first North American base for its current fields of operations in Canada by starting to sell rock excavation equipment in the Kirkland Lake, Ontario mining district in 1949. The following year it opened a more traditional headquarters in Montreal and branches in Vancouver, Port Arthur, Toronto and Truro. Edmonton and Sudbury followed a few years later. Atlas Copco has slowly and methodically expanded its North American market presence, carving out new product areas and geographic territories. The same year that the group opened its Canadian headquarters in Montreal, it also began selling compressed air equipment in the United States. In recent decades, Atlas Copco has expanded largely through acquisitions, with the ambition of becoming a market leader in each area. To take an example from the business area that first brought Atlas Copco to North America — Construction and Mining Technique — in 1993 the Robbins Company of Kent, Washington (tunnel boring and raise boring machines) was acquired. Atlas Copco had previously purchased Wagner Inc. of Port-land, Oregon (underground loaders) in 1989. Uniroc, with its drill steel factory in Ft. Loudon, Pennsylvania, is part of the same business area, as is the construction tools specialist Atlas Copco Berema Inc., West Springfield, Massachusetts. U.S. operations in the Compressor Technique business area are run by Atlas Copco Compressors Inc. in Holyoke, Massachusetts (industrial and portable compressors); they also include AC Comptec Inc. in Voorkeesville, New York (plant air and process compressors), California-based Rotoflow Corp. (natural gas expanders) acquired in 1990, and AC Rental ("oil free" air). The business area in which Atlas Copco has expanded fastest in recent years is Industrial Technique, with the 1995 acquisition of Milwaukee Electric Tool Corporation signifying a giant step into the American tool market. The Swedish company had previously operated in this market through Chicago Pneumatic of Utica, New York (acquired in 1987, relocated to Rock Hill, South Carolina in 1996) and through three companies in the Detroit area: Desoutter, Inc. (acquired in 1990), Atlas Copco Tools Inc. and Advanced Fastening Systems Inc. The North American holding company is located in Wayne, New Jersey. This account of Atlas Copco in North America may seem compressed. That is only natural, because the company operates that way: keeping up the pressure and staying efficient, as befits a company whose products have the capacity to move mountains.

The automotive industry around Detroit is an important customer category for the companies in Atlas Copco's Industrial Technique business area.

At all of Milwaukee Electric Tool's five U.S. plants, self-managed teams are responsible for production, testing and quality control.

Thanks to a 24-hour centrifugal gas compressor from Atlas Copco Comptec in Voorkeesville, NY, the National Cooperative Refinery Association's refinery in McPherson, Kansas can remove excess sulfur from its diesel fuel, yielding hydrogen sulfide — a feedstock in fertilizer production.

One of Atlas Copco's Simba drilling rigs in action at the Williams Mine in Ontario, Canada. This is familiar territory to the Swedish company, which tailored its drilling system to the conditions at this mine — the largest of three along the Hemlo Gold Belt.

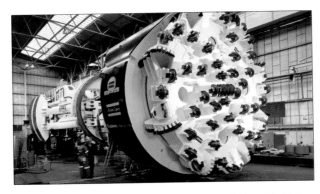

Designed and manufactured by Atlas Copco Robbins, this 23 ft diameter Robbins tunnel boring machine is being used for the Queens Water Tunnel No. 3, the largest and most costly construction project in New York City history.

The headquarters of Atlas Copco Compressors Inc. in Holyoke, Massachusetts.

The headquarters of Atlas Copco Wagner Inc. in Portland, Oregon.

Communications giant

Bo Hedfors, President and CEO of Ericsson Inc., communicates directly with customers in this advertisement photo.

In 1876, the same year that Alexander Graham Bell applied for a patent for his telephone, a Swede named Lars Magnus Ericsson started a telegraph repair business in Stockholm. This small mechanical workshop was the origin of today's huge Ericsson telecommunications group, active in 100 countries and with more than 85,000 employees. By the mid-1990s, its annual net sales surpassed $15 billion. Ericsson's largest single market is the U.S. (about 11 percent of global sales), and the Group holds nearly one third of the American market for cellular systems. Ericsson has joint ventures or strategic alliances with such U.S. companies as General Electric, Texas Instruments, Hewlett-Packard, Microsoft, Intel and IBM. But it took a long time and a lot of work to reach this point.

In 1902, Ericsson opened its first sales office in New York City. A few years later, Ericsson Telephone Manufacturing Co. inaugurated a factory in Buffalo, New York. But the

dominance of the Bell system was too strong, and in 1910 production at Buffalo shifted to automotive ignition systems. In 1923 the factory closed down. Not until after World War II, when Ericsson wanted to spread its risks by establishing production bases outside Europe, did the Group again become involved in U.S. production by becoming majority owner of the North Electric Co. (NEC) in Ohio. The two companies jointly developed the world's first electronic telephone switching system, which was delivered to the U.S. Air Force in 1962. But NEC had difficulty holding its own, and in 1967 Ericsson sold the company.

It was not until the 1980s, with the advent of cellular telephones and the split-up of the Bell system, that Ericsson made its real comeback in the American telecommunications market. Meanwhile it had established a joint venture with Atlantic Richfield Company (ARCO)

Since Ericsson took over this Lynchburg, VA factory, its operations have expanded rapidly. There are now more than 2,500 employees here, and the fully automated manufacturing line is capable of making a cellular phone every 26 seconds.

in wire and cable, as well as in communications systems, computer making and office furniture. In 1985 Ericsson bought out ARCO's interest in the venture, which by then had been renamed Ericsson, Inc. Three years later, the Ericsson Group sold its computer business to Finland's Nokia. In 1989 Alcatel bought Ericsson's cable interests.

Ericsson returned to basics in America: telephone equipment including network switching, cellular and business communications systems. And it found a new American partner — General Electric, which still holds a minority stake in Ericsson Inc., in which the Group's various U.S. operations are gathered. Corporate headquarters are in Richardson, Texas, near Dallas. Ericsson Inc.'s operations employ more than 7,000 people at about 100 locations throughout the U.S. Aside from the headquarters and training center in Richardson, major locations include a factory in Lynchburg, Virginia for the production of cellular phones, mobile radio products and systems for international markets and a new global center for digital cellular R&D in Research Triangle Park, North Carolina. Other large operations are found in Cypress and Menlo Park, California; and in Woodbury, New York. A new eastern regional headquarters recently opened in Reston, Virginia. This time around, Ericsson has a long-term strategy and is in the U.S. market to stay.

Per Nygren is Director of E-TEC, Ericsson's Technical Education Center in Richardson, TX, which is training a new generation of telecommunications engineers.

Research-intensive

Over the years Canada has evolved into a center of innovation for Ericsson, which has been active in that country since 1953. What began as a sales and service subsidiary is now one of Canada's most research-intensive companies, with more than 1,000 employees. This includes more than 700 working at Ericsson Research Canada, the new R&D center outside Montreal, Quebec. This company has the worldwide software development mandate for the CMS 8800 cellular phone system according to American standards. This product is, in turn, exported to more than 20 countries around the world, including the U.S., Mexico, Brazil, Australia, Great Britain, China and Malaysia.

But Canada is not merely an important research base for Ericsson. In the past decade, Ericsson Communications Canada in Mississauga, near Toronto International Airport, has worked very closely with Cantel (Canada's only nationwide cellular operator) as its primary network supplier, providing sales, service and distribution. By the end of 1995, Cantel had more than a million cellular subscribers in Canada and the number continues to grow rapidly.

Cantel was the first North American operator to provide coverage with new digital cellular systems. The Canadian market has been a key testing ground for this and other new Ericsson technologies. In communications systems for public safety and dispatch radio applications, the Ericsson Digital Access Communications System (EDACS) has set the standard in Canada. And SaskTel, a provincially owned telecom operator, has built the largest and most sophisticated trunked radio system in the world, with Ericsson EDACS, portable and mobile systems comprising the network. Canada will also see North America's first nationwide personal communications system (PCS), operated by Microcell and built mainly with Ericsson equipment.

Ericsson and Canada obviously get along very well with each other, despite a few occasional raindrops in Montreal.

Bernt Hoegberg, President of Ericsson Communications Canada (inset), has the privilege of working with two model facilities: the company's commercial headquarters (large photo) in Mississauga near Toronto and its new research facility in Montreal (inset below).

Inspiring headquarters in Greensboro

Volvo would never have become the world's second largest heavy truck manufacturer if it had not dared take the step into the North American market by purchasing selected assets of White Motor Corporation and setting up an entirely new base in Greensboro, North Carolina. It was one of those major strategic decisions that was not really debatable if Volvo wanted to play a leading role in the international truck market.

The transaction with White gave Volvo that company's main factory in New River Valley, Virginia — which later underwent major expansion — as well as a plant in Orrville, Ohio. Volvo also had the foresight to buy a large plot of land near Interstate 40 on the outskirts of Greensboro for its future headquarters. That is where the management of Volvo GM Heavy Truck is based today. Volvo GM Heavy Truck Corporation is the result of a 1988 joint venture between AB Volvo of Sweden and General Motors Corporation, with Volvo as the majority shareholder.

David's dream comes true

For many years, David Lee nourished a dream. He was working at Volvo Construction Equipment in Asheville, North Carolina, handling the demonstrations of the company's "big beasts": its wheel loaders, hydraulic excavators and articulated haulers for the construction, mining, forestry waste and scrap industries. And the products he demonstrated were fairly impressive. Their family histories included names like Volvo BM, Clark, Michigan, Euclid, Åkerman and Zettelmeyer. What genes! Mr. Lee was supposed to demonstrate selected representatives of this distinguished assemblage in the yard outside the Asheville factory.

Of course it was good that customers could see the quality and reliability achieved by Volvo's employee teams and by all the modern equipment at the factory. But David Lee still dreamed of a real Demonstration Center. Finally Volvo gave him the chance to realize this project. And he did almost all the work himself. Up in the Blue Ridge Mountains, at French Broad River outside Asheville, David now invites his guests to take a seat in the bleachers at the demonstration center. He turns up the volume on the loudspeakers and music pours out as the Volvo machines show off their repertoire, which is almost as smoothly choreographed as a Broadway show, David maintains.

Right: Inside the Volvo Construction Equipment factory in Asheville. Not a chance there will be a hole in this bucket.

Below: David Lee and his dream.

Dancing at the Biltmore

Generations of Americans have traveled to Asheville, North Carolina to enjoy the attractive natural scenery and pleasant climate at the edge of the Great Smoky Mountains. Close to the place where the Blue Ridge Parkway now crosses the French Broad River outside the city, the Vanderbilt family — which made a fortune in the shipping and railroad businesses — established a country retreat called Biltmore, the largest private residence in the United States. Decades later, Swedish-American poet Carl Sandburg created his last home, the beloved Connemara Farm, in the same area. But Asheville also has an active commercial life and industrial life; Swedish-owned Volvo Construction Equipment (previous page) is among the largest manufacturing plants. The more entrepreneur-driven companies in Asheville include Sweden's Q-Matic (adjacent page).

To Swedes and anyone else who travels to Asheville, the Biltmore Estate — now a historic landmark open to the public — offers a unique experience. And upstairs in the Second Floor Living Hall, Swedish visitors will discover the work of a familiar acquaintance: Anders Zorn (1860-1920), whose impressionistic painting "The Waltz" is displayed there. George Washington Vanderbilt bought the work from the artist himself at the 1893 world exhibition in Chicago. Raised in Mora, Dalarna province, Anders Zorn was the son of a German brewmaster and a Swedish peasant women, who became one of the most respected painters of George Vanderbilt's time. At Biltmore, Zorn's painting of a dancing couple captures the spirit of the Gilded Age, a period during which Vanderbilt was one of the best-known personalities.

Ticket to success

One major American market breakthrough occurred when the Atlanta Committee for the Olympic Games (ACOG) chose the Q-Matic System for its ticket sales office, downtown Atlanta accreditation center and airport accreditation office.

Every country has its own queue culture. In the United States, long lines of people are often squeezed into a small space by ropes or other barriers, thus making it hard to see how long each line actually is. In Sweden, people rarely stand in line outdoors, at least in winter, and the queue culture is generally designed to make things as easy as possible on the elderly and disabled. Modern systems of numbered tickets eliminate the need for long waiting lines and enable people to sit down, provided that seats are available. This is true at Swedish post offices, banks, shop service counters and ticket sales offices of various kinds.

The most widely used Swedish queuing system, now computerized, was created by a restaurant owner named Rune Sahlin, who felt that the lines of customers at his popular eating establishment were a bit too long. Together with his business partner Per-Martin Pettersson, he began to develop a numbered ticket system and founded Q-Matic, which has delivered some 7,000 systems worldwide.

Q-Matic entered the U.S. market in 1988 after recruiting entrepreneur Benkt Berg (right), who had just been laid off from a large U.S. corporation as Director of International Marketing. Mr. Berg had the right appetite for the task, and today he heads Q-Matic Corporation in Asheville, North Carolina, from which he markets the Swedish company's products in both North and South America. Today Q-Matic not only sells numbered ticket systems, but entire customer service management systems based on electronically stored information about customer flows and waiting times.

Benkt Berg's ultimate goal is to change the American way of waiting in rope lines to the Q-Matic computerized take-a-number system.

Vigorous 300-year-old carves new niches in the forest...

Husqvarna is one of Sweden's oldest companies. It began as a weapons foundry in 1689, only eight years after William Penn founded the colony of Pennsylvania. It took a couple of hundred years, but as we know, America eventually caught up with Europe and in many respects surpassed it. Wilhelm Tham and his son Gustaf, legendary leaders of Husqvarna for 70 years until the mid-20th century, realized that European entrepreneurs had a lot to learn from the big country on the other side of the Atlantic. During the Tham epoch, Husqvarna found its way from military to civilian production. The company's philosophy was to build up a knowledge of products "of daily help" to Swedish homes. Because the Thams wanted to create a model company whose employees lived in their own homes with gardens, this product range came to encompass products for both indoor and outdoor use.

One of Husqvarna's earliest civilian product areas was stoves. Another was sewing machines. As early as the 1870s, the Husqvarna management dispatched a young engineer, Eskil Lindblad, on a study visit to the United States. With the help of John Ericsson, the Swedish-American inventor, Lindblad gained access to

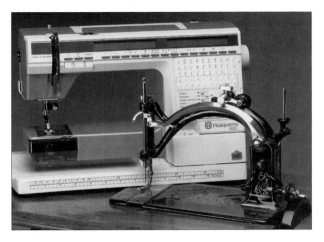

Sewing machines: As time goes by.

munitions factories as well as foundries and sewing machine plants. Husqvarna began to manufacture sewing machines on license from America's Weed company and starting in 1877 from Singer Salon. Over time, Husqvarana developed its own sewing machine models.

The Swedish company continued to expand its product range to include irons, meat grinders and other household appliances. Eventually it began to make refrigerators and freezers. Bicycles and motorcycles were added to Husqvarna's repertoire, and its knowledge of motors and engines was also applied to the production of power mowers and outboard engines. The latter led to the development of Husqvarna chainsaws.

In 1978 Husqvarna became part of the global, Swedish-based Electrolux Group. Among Husqvarna's remaining products were sewing machines, chainsaws, brushcutters, trimmers and lawn mowers. Husqvarna Forest and Garden emerged as a new product concept, and the company became increasingly adept at international marketing. The Electrolux Group, itself an expert at selling durable goods to

Husqvarna has captured approximately 10 percent of the chainsaw market in the United States and 30 percent in Canada.

... and in the garden

households, learned from Husqvarna and vice versa.

Husqvarna's forest and garden products were sold mainly through service-oriented outdoor power equipment retailers. Although the United States was a pioneer in specialty retailing chains, at the time this was not true of forest and garden products. But inspired by the American franchising tradition, Husqvarna actively built up what it calls "profiled forest and garden stores," first at home in Scandinavia, and later elsewhere in Europe as well as in the U.S.

During 1986 the Electrolux Group made two major acquisitions in the United States: the White Group, with headquarters in Cleveland, Ohio, and Poulan/Weed Eater with plants in Nashville, Arkansas and Shreveport, Louisiana. Over the next few years, Electrolux also bought such U.S.-based companies as American Yard Products and Allegretti & Co.

Electrolux grew into the world's largest manufacturer of chainsaws and a major factor in powered lawn and gardening equipment as well. While American Yard Products concentrated on deliveries to major chains, Husqvarna focused on creating a European style specialty-store base for its upscale product range. After running its American operations from Chicago for some years, in 1990 Husqvarna moved its U.S. headquarters to Charlotte, North Carolina after taking over its largest distributor. Today Husqvarna invites "forest and garden people" from throughout North America to its new base in Charlotte, where it provides training in store planning, displays its product range and coordinates its marketing campaigns.

The company may not be able to do much about the weather, but the same rains that keep people indoors when they would rather be outdoors create fast-growing lawns, bushes and trees — something that Husqvarna's forest and garden products are designed to keep in trim.

Gunder Johansson, among the few Swedes at Husqvarna's Charlotte facility, with one of the company's latest lawn mower models.

At Thomas Concrete, all stages of the delivery and service system must work perfectly in any kind of weather.

Successful mix — solid results

You would think that all the construction work that led up to the 1996 Summer Olympics in Atlanta would have set an all-time record in the order books of that city's second largest producer of ready mix concrete (market share about 27 percent). This was not the case. The order backlog of Thomas Concrete of Georgia, Inc. was actually even larger after it had completed all its Olympic-related deliveries — for example to the big track and field arena — than it was while these orders were still on its books.

So Jan Meijer (right), President of the Swedish-based concrete group AB Färdig Betong's American subsidiary, has every reason to look pleased as he stands in front of a map of one of North America's most dynamic areas.

One of life's many random events — a business acquaintance with an acquaintance who, in turn, did business in Atlanta, that got the company known today as Thomas Concrete involved in the leading commercial and industrial center of the American South as early as 1985. Otherwise, the Thomas Group's traditions as a supplier of ready mix concrete go back to 1954. The father-son team of Martin and Jan Thomas realized their company's growth opportunities outside Sweden at an early stage. The company expanded first to Germany. Later the Thomases were attracted by the dynamism they saw in Atlanta.

Today the Thomas name is visible in large letters on modern vehicles that deliver concrete to customers and distribute raw materials to the company's concrete plants in the Atlanta area. Thomas Concrete has also established a presence in Raleigh, North Carolina.

Concrete assumes its final shape and quality on the site where it is used, so quality is crucial throughout the chain from raw material through processing and delivery. Thomas Concrete has built up a network of service points and plants in and around Atlanta, all monitored via a state-of-the-art control system which provides customers with the highest quality and consistent mixes for each project.

And if you should ever end up behind a Thomas truck in Atlanta rush-hour traffic, it is comforting to know that the driver has gone through the company's own special training program. In other words, at Thomas everyone is a dedicated professional. That is why the company has been so successful.

Building new American landmarks

It all actually started in the 1960s when Skanska, Sweden's largest construction company, joined an international consortium that built several airfields in Ethiopia. The consortium also included Americans, and Skanska continued to collaborate with Americans on projects in Saudi Arabia. By 1971 the Americans invited Skanska to participate in the first subway construction project under Central Park in New York City. Skanska sent over a young entrepreneurial spirit named Claes Björk to start an American subsidiary, Skanska Inc., which is now headquartered in Greenwich, Connecticut.

The right man had ended up in the right place. Claes Björk was no desk-bound bureaucrat. He climbed down into subway excavations, visited building sites and spoke the straightforward, sometimes tough language of the construction business. The construction assignments kept coming in. In 1979 the Skanska Group became a major shareholder in the Canadian construction company Foundation, with headquarters in Toronto (subsequently divested). In 1982 Skanska bought into Karl Koch Erecting Co. in Carteret, New Jersey near New York City, a leading specialist in steel structures. Further acquisitions and partnerships followed.

Today Skanska USA is one of the 20 largest construction firms in the U.S. The company is the market leader in the New York metropolitan region and the Southeast. Aside from Karl Koch, Skanska USA includes infrastructure specialist Slattery Associates Inc., Whitestone, NY; and the program and construction management company Sordoni Skanska Construction, Parsippany, NJ. The recently acquired Skanska Engineering & Construction in Indianapolis, Indiana specializes in assignments for the chemical, pharmaceutical and other process industries. But the acquisition that gave Skanska USA what are now perhaps its most prestigious assignments can be traced back to a 1991 meeting of the Construction Industry Presidents' Forum (see next page for the other President in question).

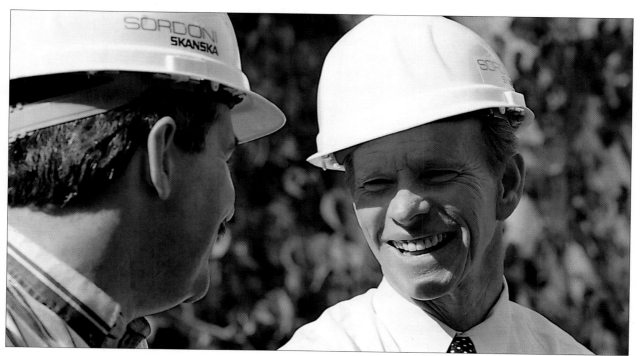

Claes Björk, President and CEO of Skanska USA, is a Swede who learned quickly how to speak the language of the American construction business.

From Gällersta to Atlanta

The man that Claes Björk met at a 1991 construction industry event was Larry Gellerstedt III, (right) whose great grandfather carried the name of Gällersta Parish outside Örebro in Sweden's Närke province to his new home in the United States during the 1840s. After living in Louisiana and elsewhere, the family eventually settled in Atlanta and established a construction business. They became major shareholders in Beers Construction Company, whose headquarters still occupies the simple wooden building (above) where the Gellerstedt family began its business. In 1994 Skanska acquired Beers.

The company has many prestigious projects behind it, among them the Georgia Dome football stadium and the Automated Guideway Transit Extension and Concourse E at Hartsfield International Airport — both in Atlanta — a recent NationsBank office tower in Charlotte, North Carolina and numerous projects in Florida. But the jewels in its crown are some 15 projects connected with the 1996 Olympic Games in Atlanta, such as the Centennial Olympic Park and the Olympic Stadium (including a contract for its post-Olympiad conversion into a baseball venue to replace the aging Fulton Stadium).

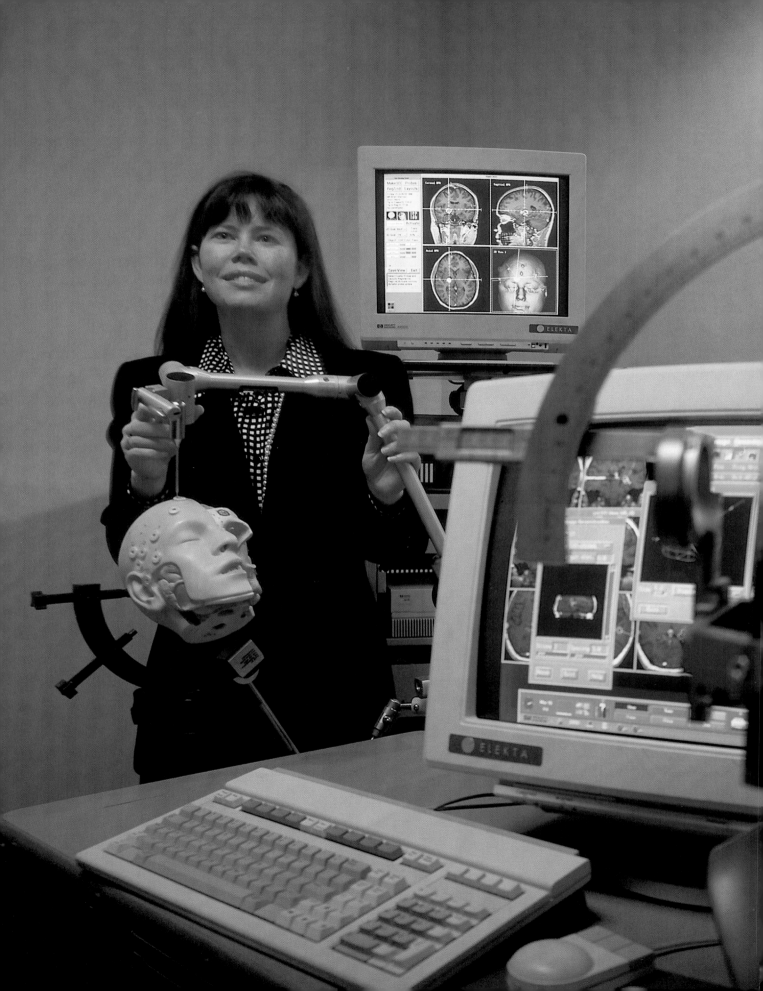

A non-invasive approach

Little did Catherine Gilmore know, when she left her home in Canada some years ago to study on a fellowship at the Stockholm School of Economics, that she was actually beginning a journey that would eventually bring her to Druid Hills, outside Atlanta. There she often lectures on a complex subject called stereotactic radiosurgery — not in the role of professor, but as President of Elekta Instruments, Inc., a company she helped build up. The reason was that one of the lecturers she met at the School of Economics was Laurent Leksell, MBA, Ph.D, the CEO of Elekta Instrument AB in Stockholm and son of Professor Lars Leksell (1907-1986), co-inventor of the Gamma Knife.®

In fact, the Gamma Knife and the new non-invasive method of brain surgery that it made possible were developed in close collaboration with American universities and hospitals. While Lars Leksell pursued his career in medical research, his Harvard-educated son Laurent became an entrepreneur who began to build up a multinational company around the Gamma Knife while teaching at the Stockholm School of Economics. The company's first market outside Sweden was, naturally, the United States. Laurent Leksell saw that one of his students, Catherine Gilmore, had the potential to help realize these plans. She was eventually appointed to head Elekta's American subsidiary, based today in Atlanta.

A product like the Gamma Knife requires instrumentation and computer support, as well as training and research related to its clinical application. Elekta Instruments, Inc.'s new sister company, Precision Therapy International in Miami, supplies software and instruments for quality assurance and dose planning in cancer therapy.

Laurent Leksell, CEO of Elekta Instrument AB.

The object that Catherine Gilmore is holding in her hand is part of the Viewing Wand,™ In the foreground is a Cartesian coordinate frame, basic component of the Leksell Micro-Stereotactic System and the Gamma Knife. It ensures that narrow beams of cobalt-60 ionizing radiation intersect precisely at the target.

Top drawer among kitchen cabinets

Gäddede in northern Sweden's Jämtland province is among the coldest spots in a country not noted for warm winters, so it is hardly surprising that when Jan Göransson (above) left his home there and moved to the United States in 1984, he chose to live in the South and continue his career in the real estate business in Atlanta.

A couple of years ago he was offered the top position at Poggenpohl's American subsidiary, headquartered in Naples, Florida. At that time, Poggenpohl, originally a purely German company, had been owned by the Swedish company Skåne-Gripen about five years and had large-scale plans for a U.S. launch. Mr. Göransson soon accepted the offer and moved to the even warmer climes of Naples.

Today Poggenpohl's U.S. headquarters have moved to a more central location in New Jersey, and Jan Göransson is back in Atlanta. From there he is directing the company's entire operations in both North and South America. The demand for its products is on the upswing. Poggenpohl sells its products via dealers and corporately owned showrooms, as well as directly to developers of upmarket condominiums and high-rise buildings. The company enjoys great brand name awareness among a sophisticated clientele — a top drawer reputation, for sure.

Poggenpohl's top-of-the-line Series 2400 kitchen, featuring high-gloss lacquered doors.

One reason why Poggenpohl located its American flagship showroom in Naples is that some of the world's most luxurious condominium developments are found here. As one real estate professional explains, "Naples personifies a refined Florida lifestyle." Many upscale buildings here are equipped with Poggenpohl kitchens as a matter of course.

He did it his way

For an entrepreneur, the desire for freedom is perhaps the most important driving force. For many years, Anders Althin held leading positions at the Swedish medical equipment company Gambro, where his father had also worked. After 15 years at Gambro, he decided to become his own boss, just like other entrepreneurs before him who had thus helped create new companies. After all, that is how industrial evolution works.

Ander Althin had already helped build up one multinational corporation. He had his contact network. Using it as a base, in 1985 he started a medical equipment sales company in Europe, Althin Medical. After five years of running his company, he was ready for the next step and bought the dialysis company CD Medical from the Dow Chemical Company. This added two factories to Althin Medical: one making membranes and dialyzers in Miami Lakes, Florida and another one making dialysis machines in Portland, Oregon. Mr. Althin moved his own headquarters to Miami Lakes, Florida. He had emigrated!

From his new American base, he began to streamline and reshape the businesses he had taken over. His wife Pia Althin also became involved in this task. Near the factory in Miami Lakes, she has established the Althin Academy, a research and teaching facility in the nephrology field with a lecture hall, laboratories, classrooms, a dialysis museum and a reference library. There is also access to an adjunct dialysis treatment unit, Miami Lakes Artificial Kidney Center, operated by the non-profit South Florida Kidney Center. So actually Anders Althin did not do it all his own way; he had at least one partner.

Perhaps one of Pia and Anders Althin's happiest moments as entrepreneurs occurred in 1995 when they opened a new factory for production of dialysis products back in Ronneby, Sweden. These entrepreneurs who had moved to America had also created jobs in their old homeland, where Althin Medical is listed on the Stockholm Stock Exchange.

Anders Althin is a man who has always liked to do things his way. His desire for independence has brought him to Miami Lakes, Florida, where Althin Medical has its U.S. headquarters and a factory. The products manufactured there include hollow fiber membranes, made by an environmentally clean method that uses no petrochemical solvents.

As in all companies that work with medical technology, safety and expert knowledge are paramount. The Althin Academy, directed by Pia Althin (right), is open to physicians, nurses, technicians, researchers and administrators in the renal care field.

A big new seller for Munters Corporation is dessicant-based air conditioning systems, which meet high indoor air quality standards. They are based on Swedish inventor Carl Munters' ingenious method for packing corrugated materials into structures with very large contact areas. In the photo (right), AC units are being assembled at the DryCool Division's new factory in Selma, Texas.

Improving the wheel

Carl Munters, founder of the global company bearing his name, was one of Sweden's innovative geniuses. In the 1920s he gained international acclaim when he invented the absorption refrigerator without moving parts together with a fellow Swede, Baltzar von Platen, as the thesis for their Master of Science degree. The invention was sold to Sweden's Electrolux group, which licensed it to the American company Servel. In the early 1930s Munters developed a foamed polystyrene plastic later licensed to Dow Chemical in the United States and used as a packing and insulation material. Dow's trademark, Styrofoam, is used today as the generic name of this material all over the world.

As part of Electrolux' license agreement with Servel, Carl Munters spent time in the United States in 1926 to help adapt the absorption refrigerator to American conditions. His visit led to a long period of cooperation with American engineers and entrepreneurs, resulting in the development of various heat exchangers and cooling contact media. In 1958 testing activities moved to Ft. Myers, Florida, where Munters Corporation was started in 1965.

One product which Carl Munters and his associates had started working on was the rotating regenerative dessicant dryer wheel. Cargocaire Engineering Corporation in Amesbury, Massachusetts, an earlier licensee acquired by Munters in 1978, developed the sorption dehumidifier, whose heart is the wheel shown on the adjacent page. In front of it is Sven Lundin, who today is President of Munters Corporation and responsible for operations in North and South America.

The latest major step in Munters Corporation's expansion was the March 1996 opening of a new plant and offices in Selma, Texas, where its DryCool Division manufactures air conditioning systems based on the dessicant dryer wheel. Munters DryCool units are found, for example, in a large number of newly constructed WalMart super centers. If you go to the refrigerated food counters, you will see small air vents on the top, from which dehumidified dry air blows out to prevent condensation and ice from forming on the food. This reduces air conditioning operating costs significantly for these stores and also provides a more pleasant atmosphere. This and similar applications at hospitals, hotels, frozen food warehouses and ice rinks have opened up a major new business area for Munters Corporation.

Golden oriole lands in Denver

The emblem of the Gylling family and their closely held corporate group is the golden oriole (in Swedish, *sommar-gylling*), a colorful bird that only rarely seizes the opportunity to visit Sweden. The Gyllings, however, seldom miss an opportunity. The founder of the group, Bertil Gylling Sr., started his own business in 1912. In the 1920s he launched the Centrum radio, later developing Centrum intercom systems into a worldwide business that was sold to Ericsson in 1967.

Around the same time, Bertil Gylling Jr. took the opportunity to become the exclusive Swedish agent of a then-unknown Japanese electronics company, Sony. The next opportunity in the Far East came in 1978, when he signed up a Korean company called Samsung. So it should not be surprising that he also launched Apple Computer in Sweden. This is the way the family has worked — taking advantage of good business opportunities that they locate through diligent research.

So when Bertil Jr. happened to hear about a new battery technology based on a spiral-wound design — SPIRALCELL TECHNOLO-GY™ — he acted quickly. In 1992 the Gylling Group bought Optima Batteries in Denver. The company's big breakthrough came in 1993, when the U.S. Air Force chose it as a prime supplier of batteries for ground equipment at its air bases worldwide. In 1995 Optima inaugurated the world's most modern factory for manufacturing automotive batteries. Meanwhile its research company Optima Advanced Technologies is working with General Motors (with funding from the U.S. Department of Energy) to develop an Optima battery to power GM's hybrid electric vehicle.

"Gylling brings technical innovations into business" is the modest credo of a company that has been showing for more than 80 years that it knows how to take good ideas and make them fly.

Bertil Gylling takes the chance whenever he can to visit the Optima factory, which is currently being expanded and will eventually produce 1.7 million automotive batteries a year.

More than 200 people work at the new Optima Batteries plant, with an area of some 100,000 square feet, located in Aurora, Colorado near Denver's new international airport.

Giving and taking

Holger Crafoord (1908-1982) spent his last school summer vacation in America, became excited about the business world and decided to become an entrepreneur.

In 1926, during his last summer vacation while a Swedish upper secondary school student, 18-year-old Holger Crafoord sailed to New York on the freighter for which his stepfather was chief engineer. He stayed a whole month. The boat on which he returned to Europe departed from Baton Rouge, Louisiana, and on the way there from New York he visited Cleveland, Cincinnati and Louisville. In his last letter before sailing home, he asked his mother when he could begin working in her Stockholm store, "because being here in the United States has opened my eyes to the fact that a business career is best." A great entrepreneurial career had begun.

Holger Crafoord played a key role in the emergence of three major Swedish companies: the packaging companies Åkerlund & Rausing

The facilities of COBE Laboratories near Denver are the Gambro Group's most important production base in the United States. From here COBE President Mats Wahlström also directs the Group's U.S. operations.

and Tetra Pak (where he was a large shareholder for years) and the company that became his own, Gambro. The latter firm was named for a Stockholm street, *Gam*la B*ro*gatan, where Mr. Crafoord had run a retail business in his mother's tradition. He created Gambro in 1964 to commercialize the artificial kidney that Sweden's Professor Nils Alwall had been working with since the 1940s. Before his death in 1982, Mr. Crafoord also planned investments in such new products as heart-lung machines.

Today Gambro is one of the world's leading companies in renal care, with close to one fifth of the global market for dialysis products. Its 1990 acquisition of COBE Laboratories in Lakewood, Colorado, a suburb of Denver, played a major role in this context. Gambro Healthcare in the U.S. includes the renal care

equipment operations of COBE as well as REN Corporation, which operates nearly 100 dialysis clinics throughout the country. Also in Colorado is the headquarters of the Gambro Group's cardiovascular surgery division — COBE Cardiovascular (CV), which has roughly one fifth of the world market for its main product, the oxygenator. Another of the Gambro Group's business areas, Blood Component Technology, is also headquartered in Colorado through COBE Blood Component Technology (BCT). The Gambro Group is a worldwide corporation whose mission is to improve the quality of life for the patients. Gambro today has about one fourth of its operations in the United States.

Lars von Kantzow, President of the Perstorp Flooring business area, moved from Sweden to North Carolina to oversee its new American venture: a new factory in Greenfield Business Park just south of Raleigh that makes Pergo, the world's best-selling high pressure melamine laminate flooring.

The right chemistry

The Perstorp Group's skills lie not only in the field of industrial chemistry, but also in the management of the human chemistry that underlies the process of technical innovation. A Swedish-based global corporation, Perstorp derives much of its strength from the way it backs the ideas and initiatives of individuals.

Perstorp's impressive expansion in North America, where it established a presence as recently as 1974, is an eloquent example. Purchasing a company in Florence, Massachusetts that produced melamine molding compounds, the Group constructed new manufacturing plants, acquired other businesses and formed partnerships that have now made the United States its largest single market. Its

As President of Perstorp Inc., Nils Lindeblad has been active in the Perstorp Group's expansion in North America during the 1990s.

American operations range from production of basic, specialty and research chemicals — at companies like Perstorp Compounds Inc. of Florence, Massachusetts; Perstorp Polyols Inc. of Toledo, Ohio; and Pierce Chemical Company of Rockford, Illinois — to specialized niche operations like R-Cubed Composites, Inc. of West Jordan, Utah and the Group's latest North American venture: Perstorp Flooring Inc. This company near Raleigh, North Carolina, makes the highly successful Pergo laminate flooring and is Perstorp's first flooring production facility outside Sweden. It also recently took over the role of world headquarters of Perstorp Flooring, the Group's fastest growing business area.

Robert V. Michel, vice president, and Richard J. Gardiner, president, are two American entrepreneurs whose joint venture with Pernovo — the Perstorp Group's business development company — has enabled them to make full use of their extensive experience in advanced composite materials. The company, R-Cubed Composites Inc., makes components for the aerospace and avionics industries such as satellite antennas, nose cones and helicopter blades at a factory outside Salt Lake City. It also makes products for such non-military applications as medicine (prostheses) and sports (race car chassis, tennis racquets, hockey sticks and golf clubs).

What a jump!

Per Welinder visited the United States for the first time in 1980 as a young skateboarding competitor. In 1982 he began a professional skateboard career around the same time that he enrolled at Western Connecticut State University. Two years later he moved west to Long Beach State University, California.

Although his marketing studies would prove important to him in the long run, during his university career skateboarding was perhaps his most important activity. In both 1983 and 1984, he was World Freestyle Skateboard Champion. He competed for Powell Peralta, where one of his teammates was Tony Hawk. After earning his degree, Mr. Welinder began working full-time for the team. At Christmas 1991, Tony Hawk and Per Welinder began making plans to start their own company, and in March 1992 they launched Birdhouse Projects Inc. from a small warehouse in Huntington Beach, just south of Los Angeles.

By the summer of 1996 they had just moved into their third headquarters in Huntington Beach and had built the world's largest skateboard ramp for their own professional competitors. In less than five years, Birdhouse has grown into the second largest skateboard company in the U.S., with additional brands such as Flip and Hook-Ups skateboards, T-shirts, hats, jeans, shoes and stickers in its product range. Birdhouse has the right graphics, the right products and the right quality. What a jump!

Christer Wernerdal and the ADBOX display system have leapt into the U.S. retailing spotlight.

Small box packs big punch

Suddenly their products were everywhere in America. But people were not talking about them. Instead they were discussing Lancôme's new perfume, Stevie Wonder's latest CD, Monet's new jewelry and Volvo's latest models. Naturally the only ones talking about ADBOX's own sales success were a small circle of cognoscenti in the promotion business.

The reason was that the above consumer products were being marketed via the ADBOX, a simple, light-weight, flexible and affordable point-of-purchase display system produced in Sweden. Christer Wernerdal, head of American operations — based in Hawthorne, near Los Angeles International Airport, since 1993 —

was of course a bit nervous when one of his biggest clients, the well-known American retailer JCPenney, sent its own people to monitor the high-quality screen printing process in Sweden, then the shipping of the folded boxes in containers. Everything went smoothly, of course, and suddenly one day: BANG. There they were in department stores all over the United States. A small box that packed a big marketing punch.

ADBOX combines the best traditions of Sweden's forest product industry (high-grade paperboard), graphic sector (screen printing) and industrial design profession (the unique way that the boxes are assembled) — and, of course, the drive of a very dedicated entrepreneur.

Apostles
of freedom

What kind of company publishes a little book that prefaces any presentation of itself with a sampling of the words of famous apostles of freedom through the ages and around the world?

It begins with Giordano Bruno — burned at the stake in February 1600 on the Campo dei Fiori in Rome by the Inquisition. Despite years of imprisonment, he refused to sacrifice his freedom of thought by recanting various scientific and philosophical theories that contradicted the 16th century teachings of the Catholic Church and challenged its moral and temporal authority. Among them was his belief that the universe is infinite and that God created many other worlds besides the earth.

The little company booklet continues by quoting the words of Abraham Lincoln in November 1863, when he dedicated part of the Civil War battlefield at Gettysburg, Pennsylvania as a cemetery for those who had died there: "We here highly resolve that these dead should not have died in vain, that this nation under God shall have a new birth of freedom, and that government of the people, by the people, for the people shall not perish from the earth."

It quotes Susan B. Anthony, a tireless advocate of women's suffrage, who condemned all forms of legal discrimination not only against women but also against black Americans. The booklet includes a statement by the Shawnee Indian leader Tecumseh to Governor William Henry Harrison during their 1810 negotiations in the Indiana Territory. It quotes an 1888 speech by jurist, diplomat and politician Joaquim Nabuco de Araujo in Recife, Pernambuco the evening before the Brazilian parliament was scheduled to decide whether to abolish slavery. And it contains a statement by Sangredo, Galileo Galilei's alter ego, in the *Dialogue Concerning the Two Chief World Systems*.

Of course this brief anthology of famous words about the nature of freedom includes excerpts from the oft-cited speech by Dr. Martin Luther King Jr. on the steps of the Lincoln Memorial in Washington, D.C. on August 28, 1963:

"So... Let freedom ring from the mighty mountains of New York. Let freedom ring from the heightening Alleghenies of Pennsylvania. Let freedom ring from the snowcapped Rockies of Colorado. Let freedom ring from the curvaceous peaks of California.

"But not only that — let freedom ring from Stone Mountain in Georgia. Let freedom ring from Lookout Mountain of Tennessee. Let freedom ring from every hill and molehill of Mississippi. From every mountainside, let freedom ring.

"When we let freedom ring, when we let it ring from every village and every hamlet, from every state and every city, we will be able to speed up that day when all of God's children, black men and white men, Jews and gentiles, Protestants and Catholics, will be able to join hands and sing in the words of the old Negro spiritual, 'Free at last! Free at last! Thank God Almighty, we are free at last!'"

Think about the above words. Ponder their significance for a while before turning the page and discovering the name of the company that evokes such wise apostles of freedom.

In service of freedom

Do you remember the first time you left home and ventured out into the world on your own to study or work somewhere else, or just to take a trip? Do you remember the sense of freedom this experience gave you?

Every successful, expansive company is based not merely on a good product or business concept, but also on feelings or sensations. To the group of companies gathered under the EF Education banner, giving the customer a sense of freedom is the sustaining theme of their operations. These companies share the goal of tearing down language and cultural barriers, enhancing personal freedom and giving individuals the opportunity for self-development.

EF stands for Europeiska Ferieskolan — Swedish for European Vacation School — and

EF's first base in North America: Santa Barbara, California.

was founded in 1965 by Bertil Hult, an entrepreneur for whom the desire for personal freedom was the driving force behind the task of building up a company. As a young student, Mr. Hult began arranging skiing trips from Sweden to the Alps. Soon he was a full-fledged tour operator specializing primarily in youth-oriented trips from Sweden to other parts of Europe. During the 1960s, thousands of Swedish young people tested their freedom by participating in the tours that Bertil Hult organized.

Arranging language-learning stays was a logical next step, but one that also carried heavy responsibilities. Bertil Hult wanted to be on the spot to see how the host families of visiting language students were being selected. He wanted to meet the teachers and help choose the schools. He spent much of the 1970s and 1980s living in various parts of Europe and the United States with his family. He spent a number of years in Switzerland building up EF in the Continental market. Dreaming of America, he decided early that during one period of his life, he would simply have to live in California.

He, too, had a dream: Bertil Hult, the entrepreneur who created EF Education.

Mr. Hult began building up the American branch of EF from Santa Barbara, California. From there he commuted during one period to Japan and established operations in the Far East. But the time difference between his Pacific

Ocean base and the large business he was running in Europe became too difficult. He relocated his American headquarters to Boston. After a time, he closed the circle by moving home to Sweden.

Today EF operates in about 40 countries. Every year some 200,000 course participants study English, German, French, Italian, Spanish or other languages under its auspices. But EF is more than a holiday language program. The EF High School Year enables secondary school students to spend an academic year studying in a foreign country. The company also operates residential language courses for students aged 18 and up. The subsidiary EF Corporate runs language institutes that offer tailor-made programs for companies large and small. EF English First is a global network of local language programs, aimed at those who lack the time or means to learn English outside their own country. EF Multimedia develops educational programs on CD-ROM. EF Au Pair is a government-regulated, nonprofit business that gives young Europeans an opportunity to live and study in the United States for one year as members of an American family.

EF's American headquarters in Boston is in charge of such programs as EF Educational Tours, which organizes trips for North American students and their teachers in more than 100 variations on six continents. This is what EF calls "The Global Classroom." It is hard to imagine a greater freedom of choice.

Olle A. Olsson is head of the EF Institute for Cultural Exchange Inc., which includes EF Educational Tours and has its headquarters in Cambridge, Massachusetts, right across the river from Boston.

In what was once a convent outside Boston, EF today operates
an international school for young people from all over the world.

A store of his own

When Björn Bayley started working at IKEA in 1969, it was a small company with a handful of popular home furnishings stores. It had just begun to expand outside Sweden — to neighboring Norway and Denmark. He joined the team that began spreading the IKEA concept of low-cost, high-value furnishings and no-frills management to other countries around the world. They started with Switzerland and Germany. Mr. Bayley himself looked forward to running the first IKEA emporium in Great Britain, but was asked to manage the company's stores in Canada instead. They had been under a franchise arrangement. The first Canadian store had opened in Halifax, followed by new units in Ottawa, Vancouver, Toronto, Edmonton, Calgary, Montreal and elsewhere.

Björn Bayley himself moved to Vancouver, where he directed IKEA's continued expansion in Canada. He quickly put down roots in that west coast city, which is among the world's most beautiful. In 1983, Vancouver also became the site of IKEA's first company-built store in North America. Meanwhile the retail chain's founder, Ingvar Kamprad, had phoned Mr. Bayley and asked him to manage its entry into the U.S. market from his base in Canada.

In 1985 IKEA opened its first U.S. store in what was once the New Sweden colony — at Plymouth Meeting, Pennsylvania, just outside Philadelphia. Of course the one thing had nothing to do with the other. IKEA had simply found a good location and good premises, so it took the plunge into a new national market. The rest is history.

For Björn Bayley, too, a new future began. After directing the U.S. expansion of IKEA from his new Philadelphia base for several years, he began to tire of all the travel to management meetings in Europe. In 1990 he relocated back to the west coast. This time he chose Seattle, where he and longtime colleague Anders Berglund were given the opportunity to become shareholders in the new IKEA store in Renton, south of Seattle. It was IKEA's first franchise arrangement in the United States.

Every morning before the Renton store opens, Mr. Bayley gathers his employees at the cash registers to review the previous day's business and upcoming activities. Perhaps this is the time of day he enjoys the most. The man who helped build up IKEA's international retail network finally has a store of his own.

Personal gallery

Decided early

While still at school in Landskrona, Skåne province, Sweden, Bertil O. Lundh wrote in an essay that by age 24 he would be living in America, where he had one relative. This was his big childhood dream. In the event, he arrived in Seattle, Washington as a 22-year-old in 1949 after completing his Swedish military service. The following year he was drafted and sent to the Korean War. He returned with a lifetime's worth of experiences. Then he began "with two empty hands" as he puts it, digging ditches for a Swedish-American contractor in Seattle. He advanced to carpenter and then became a foreman.

By 1954, at the age of 27, he was running his own construction firm. In 1990 he retired as head of Bertil O. Lundh Construction, Inc. He is a member of the nationwide umbrella organization Swedish Council of America, is a founding member of the Nordic Heritage Museum and serves on the boards of many nonprofit organizations.

Today Mr. Lundh devotes much of his time to his hobbies, one of which is fine porcelain and crystal. He owns the Porcelain Gallery, a family-operated business specializing in world-renowned artware and tabletop items in porcelain, crystal and silver. The Lundhs have two sons, Steven and Michael, and four grandchildren, who enjoy hearing grandpa tell the story of how, as a child, he dreamed of living in far-away America...

Leading ladies in California

Barbro S. Osher (left) and Siri M. Eliason (right) are both honorary Consuls General of Sweden: Barbro in Los Angeles and Siri in San Francisco. Barbro Osher's first visit to the United States occurred in 1962, when she won a scholarship with the Experiment in International Living and spent a summer in Maine. There she met the man who would become her husband 18 years later. In the meantime, she graduated from Stockholm University in languages and political science and pursued a career in the Stockholm publishing and advertising world. Since the early 1980s, Mrs. Osher has lived in the San Francisco Bay Area. She chairs the Bernard Osher Foundation — well-known for its contributions to educational and cultural causes — and commutes to the Consulate General in Los Angeles. Her husband Bernard, a cofounder of World Savings, is owner and president of the Butterfield & Butterfield auction house. Barbro Osher has played a leading role in the Swedish Women's Educational Association (SWEA) and Positive Sweden and has represented the Royal Swedish Academy of Engineering Sciences (IVA) on the west coast. In 1991 she also became owner and publisher of *Vestkusten*, a now 110-year-old Swedish-American newspaper.

Siri Eliason and her late husband Sven arrived in the United States during the 1950s from Lycksele, northern Sweden, where they had run a family furniture business. After returning briefly to Lycksele, they decided that California was for them. Settling in the Los Angeles area, they built up Scandiline Industries, an office furniture company with factories both in the U.S. and Europe. In time, Siri also built up her own business, Danica, Inc., a chain of retail stores selling mainly Scandinavian furniture. The Eliasons became active in Swedish-American cultural and business affairs. In 1984 they moved to San Francisco after Sven Eliason had been appointed Sweden's honorary Consul General. When he died unexpectedly the following year, Siri Eliason was widely regarded as his logical successor, but she was appointed to the position entirely on her own merits. Over the years she has held key positions with the Swedish-American Chamber of Commerce, SWEA and other organizations. Her tireless efforts on behalf of Sweden have led to numerous honors, and in 1996 she was named Swedish-American of the Year by the Vasa Order of America.

Both Mrs. Osher and Mrs. Eliason also serve on the boards of the American-Scandinavian Foundation and the Swedish Council of America.

Popular pastors

Johan Wierup and Susanne Forshaga-Källberg work mainly out of 5 East 48th Street in New York City, the venue of the only Swedish Seamen's Church in the United States. Organized in 1873, the church moved to its present facility in 1978. Today the church is a unique meeting place in mid-Manhattan for young adults, professionals, families, children and the elderly. Johan Wierup is a veteran pastor who assumed his post in New York in 1991, after six years as the Swedish pastor at the Norwegian Seamen's Church in San Pedro (the main port of Los Angeles). Susanne Forshaga-Källberg arrived in New York in 1995. Aside from their normal parish work and visits to Swedish vessels docked around the New York area, the two pastors are welcomed at regular intervals to lead services in Washington, D.C. (Augustana Lutheran Church), Philadelphia (Gloria Dei) and even in faraway Mexico City.

Historical roots

Parry M. Norling personifies much of the Swedish-American heritage. In 1854 his ancestors Anders Olsson and Nora Lisa Olsdotter arrived in Bishop Hill, Illinois from Nora, Sweden in the second wave of Jansonites, adopting the name Norling. By sheer chance, he now lives with his wife Nancy in the heart of the former New Sweden colony. He works as Planning Director in DuPont's Central R&D operation in Wilmington, Delaware. A graduate of Harvard College with a Ph.D. in polymer chemistry from Princeton, he has been with DuPont since 1965. Despite the generations that have passed since his ancestors arrived in America, he feels a strong Swedish heritage: "You find it in the work ethic, in a sense of seriousness and responsibility about your job," he says. Parry M. Norling drives a Volvo and has a daughter named Christine and a son named Jon.

Tracing Leif Erikson

As an archaeologist, Birgitta Lindroth Wallace is one of the world's foremost authorities on Leif Erikson and the Norse in North America. Her own first journey to America occurred when she became a young graduate fellow at the University of Kansas, having already studied Northern European archaeology at the University of Uppsala, Sweden. After marrying an American and moving to Pittsburgh in 1963, she began to work at Carnegie Museum of Natural History, which gave her the opportunity to participate in the task of excavating the recently discovered Norse site near L'Anse aux Meadows in northern Newfoundland. After moving to Ottawa, Canada, in 1975 she became a Staff Archaeologist with Parks Canada and later settled in Halifax when her position was transferred there. Ms. Wallace has published and lectured extensively on the subject of the Norse in North America, serving as a consultant to Time-Life Books, Reader's Digest, National Geographic and other publishers, as well as educational TV series. She is convinced that L'Anse aux Meadows really is the place where Leif Erikson had his American headquarters.

Preserving five heritages

Marianne Forssblad (right) is the principal creator of the world's only museum that specializes in presenting the shared cultures of all five Nordic countries (Denmark, Finland, Iceland, Norway and Sweden), with an emphasis on their Nordic-American heritage. As a young scholarship recipient, she arrived in the United States for the first time in 1959 to study political science at Hollins College, Virginia. She stayed an extra year and continued her studies at the University of Texas, Austin. After a year at home in Sweden, she traveled to Seattle and specialized in library science and Scandinavian studies at the University of Washington. This was how she began working with emigration history. When Seattle's Nordic-American colony began discussing the idea of a joint museum, Marianne Forssblad was the obvious candidate to help transform the project into a reality. The result was the Nordic Heritage Museum, located in Ballard, a neighborhood north of downtown Seattle with a historic concentration of Nordic immigrants. Don't miss it!

From MOMA to Sotheby's

Richard E. Oldenburg arrived in Chicago at age 3 when his father, a Swedish diplomat, was appointed Sweden's Consul General there. Although he received an all-American upbringing including Harvard College, Harvard Law School and the U.S. Army, Swedish was the language he spoke at home. Through his older brother, pop artist Claes Oldenburg, Richard came into contact with the art world at an early age. His publishing career at Doubleday and Macmillan led him in 1969 to a position as head of the publications department at The Museum of Modern Art in New York. Three years later he became Director of the whole museum and stayed at this post for a record-shattering 22 years. As Director Emeritus of MOMA, he has begun a new career as Chairman of Sotheby's North America. Through this venerable international auction firm and his membership on various boards and committees, he remains faithful to the world of art. Mr. Oldenburg is also an active supporter of Swedish-related causes; his awards in this field include being named 1995 Swedish-American of the Year by the Vasa Order of America.

Scandinavian gourmet

Håkan Swahn once worked as an Assistant Brand Manager at Procter & Gamble in Sweden. In 1977 he earned his degree from the Stockholm School of Economics, and in 1980 he was awarded a traineeship at the Swedish Trade Office in New York. This brought him back to the country where he had been a high school student ten years earlier (in Grand Rapids, Michigan). One of the export projects he was assigned to work with at the Trade Office involved Swedish food. It brought him into contact with Tore Wretman, an internationally renowned restaurateur and authority on Swedish culinary culture. Mr. Swahn had both an entrepreneurial flair and a genuine interest in food. In 1987, backed by a group of businessmen including Tore Wretman, he opened a restaurant called Aquavit on the lower two floors of a townhouse on West 54th Street in midtown Manhattan (complete with waterfall). It is a venue where Scandinavian design and Scandinavian food combine to create an atmosphere

that Americans like. Mr. Swahn was in the right place at the right time, with the right food. We needn't bother mentioning his talents in golf, rollerblading or marathon-running. Skål!

Swedish kids' clothing
moves west — to Japan!

Gun Denhart — a motivated and resourceful business strategist — is also a highly educated, charming woman with a social conscience. By the time she earned her MBA at the University of Lund, Sweden she dreamed of running her own company. Her changing personal life took her to Paris, then she moved to a fast-paced existence in the New York area with her new husband Tom, an advertising executive. Together they dreamed of a quieter life, with more time for family, in Tom's native Portland, Oregon. At least that is what they intended. Soon they were in Portland — way out west, only a short drive from the sea breezes and breakers of the Pacific Ocean.

Their son Christian, now a teenager, provided the inspiration for their new company. When Christian was born in the early 80s, Gun Denhart searched in vain for the kind of gentle, comfortable children's clothing of the quality she was accustomed to from Sweden. So when they moved to Portland, she and her husband started a mail order company that sold Swedish-style children's clothing. Gun Denhart borrowed her paternal grandmother's name — Hanna Andersson — as the name of the company, designed and had the clothing made, printed 75,000 catalogs, hand-glued small fabric samples into each copy in the garage at their Portland home, and advertised in American periodicals like *Parent Magazine*.

The telephones began ringing, and within a year the company became a success. Today Hanna Andersson is an established name not only in North America, but also in Japan, where they have successfully begun doing business. Down the street from the Hanna Andersson headquarters in Portland is a clothing factory that sews Hanna's designs exclusively.

Hanna's participatory management style, progressive employment benefits and philanthropic initiatives have earned it national recognition, for example the *Forbes* magazine Business Ethics Award. Caring and sharing are an integral part of Gun Denhart's personality and business style.

A professional strategist

Ulf Nilsson was one of Sweden's ice hockey exports to North America during the 1970s. His professional hockey debut took place in Winnipeg during the 1974-75 season. In 1978-79 he joined the New York Rangers, where he stayed until 1983. Finding it hard to leave the city that is the home of Madison Square Garden, he began a career in marketing Swedish products in the United States. Today he is employed by the Swedish-owned management consultant company Business Training Systems in Stamford, Connecticut. The former pro hockey strategist has become a professional developer of personnel and business strategies. And who could be better than this consummate team player at showing others how to define their own roles in a corporate team.

Good outlook

Per Karlqvist was working as an optician in Borås, Sweden when he heard that there were good prospects for his profession in North America. So he put an ad in a U.S. optical journal, got a reply from an optician in the "Swedish" city of Jamestown, New York, and moved there in 1975 with his wife Anna. After a year or so, he was offered a chance to rent a store in Chicago, and another year later he opened his own first store in Denver, Brookridge Optical. Since then, Per and Anna Karlqvist have remained faithful to Denver. Their two daughters were born and have grown up there. Per has stayed in touch with his Swedish roots, among other things by helping to establish the Swedish-American Chamber of Commerce - Colorado.

A Wallenberg ambassador

Count Peder Bonde is not only a member of a distinguished noble family with a 15th century Swedish king as an ancestor, but on his mother's side he is also related to the Wallenbergs, Sweden's leading financial and industrial dynasty for more than a century. He is a first cousin of Peter Wallenberg, the family patriarch, and a second cousin of Raoul Wallenberg, the Swedish diplomat who saved an estimated 100,000 Hungarian Jews from certain death at the hands of the Nazis during World War II.

His first extended stay in America began in 1952. At the time he was a young lawyer who had just completed his district court service in Sweden and worked for Stockholms Enskilda Bank — the Wallenberg bank, which in 1972 became part of Skandinaviska Enskilda Banken. He spent a year in New York, studying at Columbia University and later working as a trainee at the then-First National City Bank (now part of Citicorp).

Peder Bonde continued his career at the family bank and was eventually promoted to deputy chief executive officer. He has also held various other executive positions within the Wallenberg sphere, and he served as Working Chairman of the highly successful New Sweden '88 jubilee, which celebrated the onetime colony's 350th anniversary with a Swedish royal tour as well as numerous banquets, exhibitions, seminars and cultural events throughout the United States.

Peder Bonde continues to work full-time for the Wallenberg Group, now with a new focus. Since 1991 he has functioned as the Group's "ambassador" in the U.S. capital, where he lives with his wife Clarissa and their three children. He has a well-established position in Washington society and a network of contacts that stretches across the United States. He also chairs the European-American Chamber of Commerce, which represents some 80 major corporations on both sides of the Atlantic. In the photo above, Count Bonde is discussing the latest news with Bill Gates, founder and President of Microsoft.

Grand Old Man

Very few people have done as much as Franklin Forsberg to strengthen relations between Sweden and the United States. Born of Swedish parents in Salt Lake City, Utah in 1905, he served as U.S. Ambassador to Sweden in 1981-85 and played a key role in warming up relations between the two countries after the lingering memories of their Vietnam War disagreements. By then he had an exciting career behind him as a magazine publisher and communications consulting veteran, having helped create such magazines as *Madamoiselle* and *Yank*. Having celebrated his 90th birthday, he remains very active in Swedish-American circles and commutes almost daily from home in Connecticut to his New York office on Park Avenue.

Signe's star

Occasionally a heavenly star will seek its earthly dwelling in a seemingly delicate human body. One of these is Signe's star, taken from the sign of Leo (where else?). Signe Hasso brims with talent in films, theater, lyrics, music, poetry and literature. Her star shines not only in Sweden, where she was born, but also over much of Europe and all of America, not to mention the other corners of the world where her films and TV shows are seen. Yet she retains her humility, and her friends describe her as a "healer." When RKO lured her to Hollywood in 1940, she was already a celebrated, award-winning Swedish theatrical actress and movie star. She also spent time in New York, making her debut in a play that opened the night after Pearl Harbor and closed within a week. But Signe Hasso won the Best Foreign Actress award for that theatrical season and soon returned to Hollywood. After that came a movie career spanning a host of films, including "Crisis" opposite Cary Grant and "House on 92nd Street" and "The Seventh Cross" with Spencer Tracy. Her star on the Hollywood Walk of Fame was unveiled on February 1, 1994. She has also found time to write lyrics and music for Swedish jazz singer Alice Babs and others. Signe Hasso has authored numerous books — both autobiographies and novels — and has received prizes and honors including knighthoods from Sweden and Spain as well as those acknowledging her role as an "ambassador" of Swedish-American culture. "Can't believe I've done it all, but I did and Life goes on," she comments. Perhaps Singe Hasso prefers poetry above all else. One of her most recent verses:

ALPHA - OMEGA -
BEGINNING and END -
WHICH is WHICH ?
They might switch -
Become ONE -
Be the same
except for the name.

Giving something back to America

Olof Stenhammar might easily have become an immigrant in the United States, if a medium-sized Swedish company had not offered him a job as President. At the time he was working in America. The week after the first specialized options market in the U.S. started business in Chicago, Mr. Stenhammar began his first job as a licensed stockbroker at W.E. Hutton & Co. in Hartford, Connecticut. But fate called him home to Sweden.

There he made good use of the knowledge he had gained in America, by starting Sweden's first specialized options market within the framework of what is now the OM Group. Today Olof Stenhammar and OM are taking the opportunity to give something back to America. The American Stock Exchange has become the first U.S. bourse to which OM is delivering its systems technology: in this case an electronic Options Display Book System based on OM's Click Trading system.

Mr. Stenhammar, who launched OM Stockholm and OMLX (the London Securities & Derivatives Exchange) and has exported related technology and know-how to several other European countries as well as the United States, is not resting on his laurels. He has now assumed the challenging task — as President of Stockholm 2004 AB — of attracting the 2004 Olympics to the scenic Swedish capital, which hosted the 1912 Games.

Focusing on the future

Imagine a world where cars are exhaust-free and where coal- and oil-fired power stations have largely been replaced by generating plants that collect solar energy directly and transform it to electricity or other forms of power.

That reality may be closer than you suspect, if General Stirling Inc. is on the right track. Lennart Johansson, President and CEO, is working in the present but, as he says, "focusing on the future." His company's efforts are being closely followed by such heavy hitters as General Motors, the National Renewable Energy Laboratory, Science Applications International Corporation, the Department of Energy (DOE) and Sandia National Laboratories. Obviously someone like Lennart Johansson who works on the cutting edge of such new

technologies as exhaust-free engines and transformation of solar energy attracts a lot of attention.

Why has Lennart Johansson, born in the 1940s in the small Swedish city of Södertälje, ended up in the energy technology spotlight? Let's take a brief look at his story.

As a young student, Mr. Johansson began working in the engine shop of Scania, a truck manufacturer in Södertälje, Sweden, where his father was a foreman. Lennart loved working with large diesel engines — just as he had enjoyed playing with steam engines as a child. His dedication to motors and engines was so great that after graduating from engineering school, he worked for FOA, the Swedish defense research institution, and later for the government-owned defense company FFV. There he was involved in the development of the most exciting engine he had ever encountered: the Stirling engine. This ingenious external combustion engine converts any form of heat into mechanical power. The Stirling cycle machine originated in Philips Laboratories in the Netherlands several years ago. The Swedish group acquired a license from Philips and further refined the engine.

Mr. Johansson was asked by his Swedish government-owned employer to explore the potential market for Stirling engines in North America. He established a small company in Ann Arbor, Michigan, where he continued development work. One day, he found himself with a new employer, when "his" American company was sold by the Swedes to McDonnell Douglas. But after only a few years, the big U.S.-based group decided to focus on its aircraft business. This gave Lennart Johansson his big chance. He lined up strong — very strong — financial backing and formed General Stirling Inc., with its subsidiaries Stirling Thermal Motors, Inc. (STM) in Ann Arbor and Stirling Cryogenics & Refrigeration (SCR) in the Netherlands. The latter company has developed and sold reliable equipment for the production of liquid nitrogen and oxygen. Put simply, it uses "reverse" Stirling technology to create cold instead of heat.

Stirling Thermal Motors took the original concept and completely re-engineered it into a compact, efficient, clean engine. Today STM is the recognized technology leader worldwide with its new Stirling engine, which can be manufactured at a competitive cost compared to conventional internal combustion engines. General Motors has evaluated the company's engine and decided to use it exclusively in the DOE/GM hybrid electric vehicle (HEV) program. One advantage of this engine is that it can be used with different kinds of fuel, including petroleum, and thus requires no major change in today's filling station network. The fact that exhaust system manufacturers have become involved in General Stirling may perhaps be viewed as a prudent measure on their part for the future. The STM engine needs no muffler or catalytic converter.

It will take many years, however, before Stirling engines are widely used in conventional cars. The development costs are steep, and the first commercial Stirling engines will be delivered for industrial and military applications rather than for consumer products. The engines can also be used in new markets like solar/bio-mass-fueled power conversion systems and HEV power plants.

Such new Stirling Thermal Motors products as the STM 4-120 four-cylinder multi-heat engine — which converts any form of heat into either mechanical or electrical power in an environmentally friendly way — are being spearheaded by a man who grew up surrounded by engines, in the shadow of a truck factory. And what is Lennart Johansson's hobby? The answer is horsepower, but of a different and even more natural variety. He keeps several horses in the countryside not far from his Ann Arbor home and often takes long horseback rides across the forests of Michigan, the part of America he has chosen as his home. After all, this is where the world's largest aggregation of knowledge about engines and vehicles can be found.

It will take years to perform the necessary long-term tests that are required before Stirling engines can be launched in the marketplace. The energy that these test engines generate is sold to the local power grid.

In Golden, Colorado, Stirling Thermal Motors is testing its Solar Power Conversion System in a three-phase joint venture program co-founded by the U.S. Department of Energy (DOE) and industry. DOE's Sunlab, staffed by Sandia National Laboratories and the National Renewable Energy Laboratory (NREL), is providing technical assistance to STM in design analysis and testing.

CORPORATIONS

PERSONAL GALLERY

PHOTOS

BLOMÉDIA AB, 1996
ISBN 91-972580-9-1